5/10/73

YEAR
ONE
CATALOG

YEAR
ONE
CATALOG

A Spiritual Directory for the New Age

Edited by Ira Friedlander

Introduction by Pir Vilayat Inayat Khan

1817

HARPER & ROW, PUBLISHERS
New York · Evanston · San Francisco · London

CONTENTS

This book is dedicated
to all teachers,
known and unknown,
who have been and are
channels for His Light

ACKNOWLEDGMENTS

Palms together I would like to thank Barbara Friedlander, Hadya, Marilyn Mark, Charlene Morgan, Victoria Tarlow and Susan Weitzman for their help and kindness in producing this book.

Blessed are you that are so wise!
Blessed am I that I have fallen into your company.

TRIPURA RAHASYA

Editor's Note: If your center is not listed in this book and you wish to be listed in the next edition of the *Year One Catalog,* send details about yourself or your organization to me at the Harper & Row Religious Books Department.

The descriptions contained in these entries, in most cases, have been provided by the centers and organizations themselves and do not necessarily reflect the viewpoint of the editor.

FOREWORD

In the New Age man has come to realize that he must be more than a cosmic apparatus for the transformation of food. He must become a cosmic apparatus for the transformation of Light.

Consider this book as a series of spiritual pumpkins that you can explore and taste. Spiritual pumpkins grow in any weather and are growing more now in America than ever before. A great spiritual energy has been moved to this country and holy men of the East are following it, and, of course, they bring the Light within them to become our mirrors. They establish centers or "ashrams" and reconfirm the spiritual centers within ourselves. They plant the seeds of inner peace with their Divine Grace, which remains and nourishes like a good rain that falls on fertile soil; long after the rain has gone, the seed in the soil continues to grow.

There is a tremendous aspiration among the youth of this country and sincere seekers are drawn to sincere teachers. Those who are curious sometimes only need a little more information and attention to become sincere.

We are like light bulbs. All of the energy and electricity is within us and the wiring is complete, but we do not know the location of the switch; and because the Light has not passed through the bulb in a long time, its surface has accumulated many layers of dust. The Guru, or spiritual teacher, turns the switch on, approaches the bulb, and cleans a little spot. Immediately we feel different, as if we have been washed with Light. Now it is our job to continue dusting.

May His Light All Ways Pass Through You.

IRA FRIEDLANDER

**YEAR
ONE
CATALOG**

PIR VILAYAT INAYAT KHAN

❝In meditation, the will seems
to be more free to attune
consciousness from one
state of reality to another.❞

Introduction:

LAUNCHING INTO THE NEW AGE!
by Pir Vilayat Inayat Khan

Sensitive minds throughout the planet nurture the hunch that something of moment is happening. Old-timers are shocked to see how fast old values are being discounted and accepted forms ditched, and how recklessly the old order, built at the cost of so much human endeavor, is being baffled without the slightest compunction or fear for the morrow by new-styled people who live joyfully, sometimes with rapt intensity, and are afoot on a frantic quest for meaningfulness. Young people from all corners of the globe and all walks of life, including "young people of all ages," seem to be kneaded by some uncanny fashioning process into a pattern of nonconformism that looks sometimes very much like a new and rather bizarre conformism, or at least "conformism to nonconformism." These idealists, whose realism is sometimes disconcerting, refuse to become dollar-making machines; they mean to build a world of beautiful people rather than conveniences, admittedly sometimes forgetting that such a luxury is a by-product of the affluent society upon whose shoulders it rests.

Yet these young people have a flair for things to come; although their ways and means are being improvised with trial and error, their stamina will not be discouraged by setbacks or apparently unsolvable hurdles. Each civilization stands on the backs of its predecessors and is thus enabled to envision new solutions that escaped their predecessors' intuition. The forward march of civilization is so inexorable that unless one knows how to promote change, one is bound inevitably to regress and this must needs be bold, even foolhardy. It seems to be the prerogative of youth since time immemorial, for youth is inclined to take the chance of losing rather than lose the chance of winning (to borrow an expression from a prophetic pioneer of the New Age, Hazrat Inayat Khan); to try to find a way of materializing an ideal, like the youthful pupils of Pythagoras, Socrates, and Plato. Dalliance in the products of the Industrial Revolution seems to fix one in one's ego as one grows older, countering one's growth by the phenomena of fossilization, unless one knows the vade mecum of eternal youth: selflessness.

Astrologers are not of equal mind as to the exact moment of the advent of the Aquarian Age. To be precise, it is supposed to be situated on the dawn of the day of the spring (vernal) equinox of the year when the sun dawns for the first time in the constellation of Aquarius, having passed over the threshold separating Aquarius from Pisces. How this boundary is assessed seems to be a matter of approximation unless one assumes that each constellation must be separated from its adjacent ones by a rigorously equal increment of 30 degrees.

Furthermore, one has to account for the "precession of the equinoxes" owing to the increasing tilt of the axis of the planet Earth toward the sun. Sidereal astrologers since the time of the Egyptians and Assyrians have contended that this draws the influence of the new constellation to the Earth at an earlier date calculated as a constant increment. Thus, if the estimated date of the vernal passage of the sun from Pisces to Aquarius is predicted by some schools for the year A.D. 2370, it looks as though, increasingly, the influence of Aquarius is being felt already by the forerunners of the great new venture.

While the influence of the tail end of Pisces to which we are still being subjected enhances the motherlike Neptunian mystical atmosphere of the spiritual revival of our time, manifesting as a certain type of New Age person who does not seem to incarnate entirely, the prefiguring influence of Aquarius gives pioneering temperaments the more realistic, clear-sighted Uranian concern to devise ways and means of mastering matter in the service of spirit. For example, they design a new way of practical living in keeping with the harmony of the spheres, seeking in the bonds of men contracted in a spirit of freedom a "world brotherhood in the Fatherhood of God," to borrow words coined by Hazrat Inayat Khan, to define the message of our time.

Consequently, it appears as though the *raison d'être* of some spaced-out young people is simply to demonstrate the angelic condition on earth as a model for New Age man to work into the more genial type in preparation in the cosmic blueprints somewhere in those architects' offices up there.

Inevitably, New Age enthusiasts are the target of the old adage, "there is nothing new under the sun." Yet history seems to be studded with traumatic phases of change alternating with periods of relative stability for consolidation, and evolution proceeds by leaps and bounds somewhat like the physical phenomena accounted for by the quantum theory. Crisscrossing stresses jam and stalemate into stagnancy until a fresh impulse offsets the unstable equilibrium precariously reached, forcing one into new ventures, reviving the sense of purposefulness by upsetting one's complacency and security.

This is what is happening to us upon the annunciation of the Aquarian Age: We have a sense of being privileged in witnessing an advance into great happenings counterweighted by a nagging panic of impending disaster. Psychics sound the alarm, and every now and again in mass communication we are given a warning about what we are doing to the planet. Our ability to harness matter to serve our desiderata would give us the overconfidence of the apprentice sorcerer if we were not protected by our awe of the enormity of the implications of our reckless intervention in the course of nature. Atomic experiments performed by scientists and engineers with their tongues in their cheeks hang upon us like the sword of Damocles, for we realize that they know that they have no idea of the extent of the implications of their soundings in the fabric of the universe.

Such things as the shortage of water and cultivatable land in view of human consumption at large bring us face to face with the basics of life on the planet. Biology has reached a stage that places us at the mercy of those in whose hands the secrets of research may fall, for there is nothing to prevent unscrupulous people from flooding the land with four-headed monsters or toxic gases or lethal radiations. We do not know how far nature is able to protect herself from such aberrations, since we have upset the natural economy of her balance. The more one wrests the secrets of phenomena, the more one becomes conscious of the ethics of science, so that New Age man stands in awe before the preestablished order of the divine harmony in the stars as in the atoms as in the cells as in the mind. To some scientists, science leads to glorification: This is part of the New Age.

We are beginning to be sensitive to the planet as a living being and the New Age brings an awesome sense of our responsibility toward her. The prospects of catastrophe attendant upon overpopulation, pollution, deforesting, nonorganic foods, political brainwashing, religious fanaticism, and many other pathological symptoms of our time are brought home to us at our very doorstep. We know well what they point to: "That means you."

Withal, the New Age is staring us in the face, egging us on to new ventures. The more challenging the problems, the more scope there is to building a better world. The old solutions have collapsed and shown their worth. We have to find new solutions, and New Age people are on the lookout for new ways. Some ask themselves whether the television set, the availability of a telephone and an elevator and a tape recorder or a modern kitchen are worth the drudgery of the typewriter pool and the factory conveyor belt—or of what use the doctorate of that fellow who cannot find a job with it—while we are staking our health and nerves in cities that have become unlivable, segregating ourselves from the basic things such as the good earth, water, and air and real food and real human beings. The school dropout is sometimes a wise person who refuses to be duped by outdated values and wishes to be creative.

Education seems like a mounted mechanism with a certain type of society in mind; consequently, creative minds ask themselves: Why not build a system of education at the measure of the future society? Do we have a hunch as to what the future society will be like? One might infer from New Age trends that there is undoubtedly a decentralizaton from the cities forthcoming and more specifically a return to mother earth, to organic foods, dechlorinated water, natural fertilizers, herbal medicines, and so on.

If the planet has reached a stage at which the Aquarian influence comes in a timely way to weave its meshes into a meaningful pattern, imminent changes in the structure of society are naturally making themselves felt amongst the pioneers. The protective exclusiveness of the family circle is being invaded by the pressure of the agrarian instinct of Aquarius. It is a manifestation of the insecurity of our time. In an emergency, a society tightens its ranks, people draw closer and pool their resources. Group consciousness is now crowning the peak of individual consciousness reached through the Industrial Revolution as a stepping stone to point omega. "Together we are one" is the slogan of the New Age. People indulge in sensitivity group experiments, love-ins; the barriers, having been displaced, sometimes removed, overshoot the mark of the safe norm in a laxity in the unwritten laws of married life that has every reason to conjure up alarm, particularly when it reaches the point of indiscriminate promiscuity that runs the risk of rousing, by exposing the inexperienced or innocent, a regression into primitive deviations of what is a holy sacrament, the cosmic rapture of joy in the flesh, by perverting the creative instinct into a Machiavellian hell of selfish, sacrilegious, ruthless, and scornful desire. Nevertheless, a sure instinct preserves most people from deviations that violate their sense of integrity and of the divine harmony of all creation.

No doubt people drawn together by the forces of affinity are seeking to coalesce their lives into such organized though free structures as will enable them to maintain the family cell and at the same time have the advantages of a richer sharing of social life: coordination of their activities, the pooling of experience and such conveniences as a communal kitchen (at best noncompulsory), taking turns at baby sitting and at facilities where children play together, a community library, community singing and dancing, discussion or debates, and a meditation group. Though experiments in community living have not always been successful, they point the way to composite structures toward which society in the New Age will inevitably be evolving. Experience shows that they are more likely to be successful if they gravitate around an inspiring and if possible benevolent leader who gives the commune or community a sense of purpose for which adherents will give precedence to their personal wants. It is difficult to carry it off on a foot of equality, on a purely democratic basis, as individuals will tend to pull in different directions. As selfless leaders are rare, such human groupings may find it difficult to stay together after their death.

The transition into the New Age is like passing through a critical age of puberty into a newly acquired maturity. Breathtaking perspectives evidence a new awareness developing among a few who form the spearheads of the thinking layer of the planet; yet it is having a snowball effect. Humanity is acquiring a new consciousness of itself as a composite being. We are witnessing the "formation of a consciousness of consciousnesses at the summit of the universe," called point omega by Teilhard de Chardin in the New Testament of the New Age, *The Phenomenon of Man*. We are able to see ourselves as contributing toward it personally in our communications with the thinking of our fellow men in a world become smaller by the increase of the flux of ideas, awareness, and know-how.

The conquest of outer space, popularly known as the chief characteristic of the Aquarian influence, as a fixed air sign, is actually simply a symptom and corollary of the properly Uranian exploration of the far reaches of the mind. From the moment that we stumbled upon a new vantage point (the moon) from which to scan Earth, we were unwittingly faced with a new way of thinking of the planet and consequently of ourselves as the object contemplated instead of the contemplating subject: that is, with the objectivity gained when one cross-examines what one had always imagined to be one's subjectivity with a clarity born of detachment. The new stage reached by consciousness in New Age optics makes it now possible to watch the forward march of evolution and see ourselves, not only as part of it or as the spearheads of its forward thrust, but as the procession of evolution itself—evolution taking stock of itself.

For where does "us" or "we" or "I" begin? What we call our bodies are a proliferation of our parents' cells surviving dissolution by their interfusion and the chain regresses back into the unknown. Something of what we call me and you was present in the dimly felt stirrings of the protozoa, the most rudimentary living cells, or even in that nostalgia knitting the atoms into molecules called affinity, or the apparently blind impulses within the electrons that we call energy; and our memory conducted into the unconscious may unearth recollections of the music of the spheres and angelic lives. In the new perspectives, the sense of individuality tends to fulfill itself in a higher integrating dimension, enabling us to see ourselves as an unbroken continuity within change, a stream of fleeting eddies, so utterly merging into the next in the series that we wonder how we could have thought of ourselves as a phase without being the totality of which we had envisioned ourselves to be a phase.

Zeroing in on the planet Earth from the moon's-eye view brings home to us what we have been missing by wrapping ourselves in our immediate surroundings, taking so seriously our storms in our teacups while missing the big show: the choreography of the stars, the giddy whirling of the electrons within the atoms, or the flow of sap in the plants, the pulsing of the magnetic fields of all living beings, the twinkling of an aura, or the wonder of celestial spheres transpiring through a transfigured human countenance.

Our awareness is not only gaining new fields of physical reality by being supplemented with the telescope, microscope, spectroscope, stethoscope, voltameter, and electroencephalogram, but the New Age optics are able to nurture the hunch that reality may disclose itself infinitely more richly if we were to displace the vantage point internally from its orbit within body consciousness into its setting in what is known as dream consciousness, or even higher still by letting go of one layer of consciousness and letting another take over one that includes the former. Contemplatives of different faiths or schools claim to have an experience of higher strata of reality, and ESP is the latest fad on the American bandwagon (apart from the Jesus revival).

Universities have opened their doors to laboratory research on telepathy, and more or less clandestine schools on astral travel attract genuine curiosity while shedding by the roadside those who have lost their sense of reality; psychic societies and some scholars are busy collecting genuine evidence. We learn that Russian pilots are trained in ESP, presumably in case of an uncanny technical hitch (one never knows these days). Doubtless an extension of awareness to twilight states seems to be part of the new horizons gained by the advance of consciousness of New Age man into what used to be dismissed as uncanny hunches. Yet the more serious seekers refused to be sidetracked from their ultimate objective: higher consciousness, or illumination led by the intuition of a transfigured experience of the moving scene of life where all makes sense.

Doubtless the drug scene contributed toward the landslide for meditation and rocketed the whole New Age trip. Massive sections of the young in the United States and elsewhere, including an overwhelmingly large percentage of teen-agers, have been affected by it. Psychologists and physiologists have studied the attendant transformation in the sense of reality, the sense of personality, and the levels of consciousness geared into action by hallucinogens and psychedelics, and studies attempted at universities have outlined levels of experience and established parallels with psychological states or even planes of reality referred to in the *Tibetan Book of the Dead*. Having once tasted of the dazzling effulgence, uncanny liveliness, and spaceless and timeless transfiguration of the ordinary landscape of the universe that now appears like a play of shadows and puppets, the bewondered subject is said to have had his mind "opened" and needs no philosophical convincing to make him believe in the existence of higher strata of reality and will always long to experience it again.

Needless to say the use and particularly abuse or overuse of the drug is fraught with drawbacks. The drug carries one the way it will or programs for one, and should one resist or not be prepared for the traumatic shock of the difference of outlook, images are distorted into unsightliness, or one may be sucked into an annihilation vortex; fright will petrify one into a psychological cul de sac from which there is no escape, not knowing that it is the thought of being confined that confines one: it is all in the mind and so one experiences one's everyday beguilement into the hoax of maya. Drug users have a phrase for the fear of being trapped and unable to retrieve normal perception: "freaking out."

More lasting is the fact that one is faced with dimensions of reality for which one is not ready, that one is not strong enough to assimilate, whose richness the pigeonholes of our ordinary *imago mundi* (picture of the world) is unable to accommodate. The mind is "blown," unable to cope with the vastness, the splendor, the nonphysicalness, the spacelessness, timelessness, and transcendence; and when returned to normal perception, the psyche is at loggerheads to reconcile these apparently incompatible vistas of the same reality, and one's spiritual high is violated and flaunted by the harshness of ordinary people in their ego-consciousness without any protection whatsoever.

The most serious drawback comes later as a heavy bill to pay, sometimes devastating, depending upon the number of trips, the type, quality, and purity of the herb or acid, and the resistance of the subject, which is unpredictable and may vary from zero to infinity. Since it is known that the physiological functions in the brain are an incredibly intricate, delicately balanced electrochemical phenomenon a billion times more subtle than the world's most elaborate computer, one can imagine what devastation lies afield in a brain tampered with by hard drugs. The battlefield of the New Age revolution is strewn with burnt-out cases, the unwitting victims of an experiment into the unknown carried sometimes to the irreversible point of no return. Fortunately, the power or recuperation of the brain is something near the miraculous, and New Age people are turning toward meditation to meet the psychological demand triggered off by the drug.

In meditation, the will seems to be more free to attune consciousness from one state of reality to another; only in trance is one trapped on a plane and that is psychic or occult, not spiritual. In meditation the adept is trained to take a gradually wider and encompassing load of awareness and incorporate these in his mental grasp of the meaningfulness of the universe; further, he is protected by the vesture of detachment.

A pressing need to conduct experience beyond the humdrum confines in which we have imprisoned ourselves impels young people and pioneers to seek in meditation nothing less than the ultimate: awakening. The New Age seems to have triggered off a tidal wave of interest for meditation, incongruous and alarming to those (often their parents) used to the common coin gained through the Industrial Revolution. The reaction to the Sunday school at the doorstep may lead to a flight from the security of the family fold or to the flouting of the one-time coveted career for mass exodus to improvised ashrams in remote places, mostly uncomfortable, which may end in adhesion to some outlandish indoctrinization even more dogmatic and sectarian than the one left behind. But this is a feature of the New Age, for the world is welding itself into a whole, and inquiring young people are unwittingly conscripted by some unknown planner to weave these many-splendored threads that are the remains of the harvest of the great world religions into a converging pattern.

Many would not hesitate to knock at the doors of the Hindu Rishis, the Buddhist Bikkhus or Lamas, the Zoroastrian Maggi, the Jewish Hassidim or Kabalists, the Christian monks or evangelists, or the Moslem dervishes in their quest for this most precious of all knowledge, for they are weary of theories and ideas and something in them tells them that there are among these some who have the know-how leading to actual experience. This is the "do-it-yourself" age, and New Age people have become most realistic in refusing to be taken in by empty words and make-believe.

Young students will take the plunge unconditionally in the schooling of their choice yet will see nothing incongruous in combining the traditional methods of different schools or exchanging these methods between each other, while their teachers remain attached to the security of their pigeonholes. They will flock to the feet of traditional or self-styled teachers, and there has been a real exodus to the far shores of India in the "guru hunt." Many pass within a few feet of the haunts of great masters, not knowing their hideouts—they ask one not to reveal their whereabouts—while there is much display to the point of bland dramatization amongst the lesser ones, particularly in a flurry of charlatans, for spirituality is fast becoming the East's best export. Most seekers seem on the whole to be protected by a real flair for authenticity and often return disappointed in the teachers they encountered while there were authentic schools at their doorstep. "There is a place where you cannot reach by going somewhere," said Buddha.

Enthusiasts and promoters throughout the world organize jumbo mass meetings of New Age teachers. The newly clinched exchanges between these seem to catalyze a New

Age approach to spirituality. For, indeed, there are New Age methods of meditation: for example, a method advocated in the Buddhist jhanas to overcome identity with the body consists in dismissing the body as being made of earth, water, and other materials, and perishable, subject to decay; in New Age meditation, the body is not dismissed as "not me," but envisioned as a phase in an advancing procession of evolution, matter in a process of genesis "from the atom to the cell and from the cell to the organism, and from the organism to the mind," from the inorganic, through the first albuminoids, and the first outburst of reflexive consciousness, to higher consciousness—"from the geosphere, through the biosphere to the psychosphere and beyond into the noösphere: One single process: the inexorable march of evolution gains ever-new zones, launches into ever-fresh horizons. Crowning the vertiginous march, evolution reveals its 'inside' as luminous consciousness, at the same time the springboard and spearhead gain new zones of reality." In these new ways of meditating, reflecting Teilhard's vision, one finds oneself at the same time as part, though not as a portion, of the planet; not merely as body, but at all other levels of which one might be aware, yet at the same time "the visitor from outer space" that is a transterrestrial element accruing to the planet that unfolds itself by converging and interfusing the entire universe at all levels upon and within itself. For to unfold its latent potentialities the planet Earth must be fecundated by drawing the entire universe at all levels of being into its fabric, both physical and mental interfusing with the elements thus accruing to it. And are we not the antennae or aerials and at the same time the extraterrestial elements that pass through the antennae to the fabric of the planet?

The genius of Aquarius spurs New Age consciousness to an unmitigating, relentless inquiry into the harmonic order that has converged the universe into our making, the patterns that have determined the genesis of all living things through the unfolding of time, the laws of karmic causality. Inquiring minds intuit laws of causality behind phenomena, wrench meaning from appearance; the scientific mind rises from the contingent to the general. It has invaded much uncharted territory and the same indomitable will that will bypass concepts taken for granted since time immemorial to break into new dimensions of thought like non-Euclidian geometry, imponderables in mathematics, or antimatter in physics is more than ever in search of the miraculous by exploring the states of consciousness and their corresponding scale of sphere or level of being. The instruments of this investigation are a mind trained in meditation, a sensitivity keyed up to the point of identifying with that aspect of one that is nonsolid, nonspatial, timeless, effulgent, all-encompassing, the ability to conduct consciousness beyond the point where it is the consciousness of an "I."

Such a knowledge, "called transcendental knowledge" by Buddha, has been considered perennially by the unbroken esoteric traditon as an awakening. If Vedanta and diurnal (everyday) consciousness appears as a dream to the one who "awakens" into what appears to be ordinary consciousness, then from there into the greater awareness that appears to the ordinary consciousness as dreamless sleep, and so to everhigher realms, beyond the horizons of the mind passing from one celestial sphere to the next beyond the created or the perceived into beyond the beyond.

The aspirations of all religions converge at this level. Religious leaders who carry the responsibility of guiding billions of souls know that to remain segregated in their isms is tantamount to staying out in the cold, for the inexorable advance of religious awareness presses on to conjugate the forces of faith. It starts with religious good neighborhood, exchange of ideas, religious tolerance, and rapprochement promoted by world congresses of faiths leading to the fellowship, even communion, of religious leaders breaking bread at the same table, reaching an apotheosis in celebrating prayers at the same altar or sharing a meditation. However most leaders will stop short of the idea of the Overchurch integrating all religions, yet some will warm to the Universal Worship launched by the farsighted vision of those in advance of their time, yet anticipating the future. "The day will come, when the men of all faiths will unite in their prayers," said Hazrat Inayat Khan, speaking of the message of our time and representing the masters, saints, and prophets of all times who form the spiritual hierarchies of the government of the world. One wonders sometimes to which religion God belongs!

There comes a time when one is disconcerted by the insignificance of one's man-made altar or the a priori of the forms of one's ritual and the narrowness of one's dogmas, when one is shattered by the discovery of the immensity of the cosmos in all its dimensions and the remoteness of the horizon of one's highest ideal and the uncanny immanence of the Presence one had so anthropomorphized. At those rare moments New Age man awakens to the discovery of the breakthrough of the forces of life passing through him linking him to the harmony of the spheres. Then he lives the way his higher consciousness participates in the high mass celebrated in the heavens where all the heavenly hosts, archangels, angels, genii, and beings known and unknown celebrate a paean of glory and magnification. At those moments he realizes that no altar would be of the dimension of this hosanna other than the altar of the stars.

NEW YORK
AND VICINITY

AGNI YOGA SOCIETY

The Agni Yoga Society was founded by Professor Nicholas Roerich and Madame Helena Roerich. Its purpose is to spread the Teachings of the East, words of wisdom from the Great Source sent to man as a compassionate aid in his striving toward perfection.

Agni Yoga, also known as "The Teaching of Living Ethics," proclaims an undeferrable mission for mankind: to create a bridge leading to the Blessed Hierarchy. For this achievement the Heart is affirmed as the saving force and as the link with the far-off worlds.

The Society publishes and disseminates the Agni Yoga, which is the yoga given for this period in humanity's history, the New Age. Agni Yoga is the synthesis of all previous yogas, such as Raja, Jnana, and others. It embodies the great features of each yoga, blending all and giving additional knowledge for this period in history.

Agni Yoga has been given by the Hierarchy (Great Brotherhood). Anyone interested in studying it should read the books published by the Society, which must be read in consecutive order. Any questions arising from reading the books can be answered by writing to the Society.

Members may be accepted after one to three years of serious study from the books. The Esoteric Group meets twice a month. The meetings are not open to the public.

There are many groups organized throughout the country to study these books; you can learn of them by contacting the Society in New York. The books of Agni Yoga have been translated into many foreign languages and may be obtained from the Society directly or from specialized bookstores throughout the country.

The Nicholas Roerich Museum is housed at the Society's New York office. It contains many of Professor Roerich's paintings, offers exhibitions of other artists, and is open to the public Sunday through Friday.

For additional information write to the Agni Yoga Society, 319 W. 107th St., New York, N.Y. 10025.

ANANDA ASHRAM—THE YOGA SOCIETY OF NEW YORK

Ananda Ashram, opened in July 1964 by the Yoga Society of New York, Inc., is a center for the investigation and practice of the science and philosophy of Yoga. It provides a place to live, work, and study for the serious student of Yoga.

The Ashram is located near Monroe, New York (approximately 50 miles from New York City). Under the guidance of Dr. Rammurti S. Mishra, the spiritual director, the student of Yoga will attend lectures, group meditation, and classes in Hatha Yoga. In addition, many activities and community projects serve a wide range of interests. A small theater offers programs for adults and children and there are regular classes in mime, ballet, painting, and sculpture.

The Yoga Society of New York, Inc., a nonprofit, tax-exempt organization, was founded in 1957 by Dr. Mishra. At the Society's New York headquarters, lectures and Hatha Yoga programs are given several times a week and are open to the general public. The New York Society is closely affiliated with Yoga societies in Syracuse, Providence, Boston, Dayton, and Montreal. A monthly bulletin is published and distributed by The Yoga Society of Syracuse.

For further information contact Ananda Ashram, Sapphire Rd., R.D. 2, P.O. Box 212–C–1, Monroe, N.Y. 10950; (914)783–1084; or The Yoga Society of New York, 100 W. 72nd St., New York, N.Y. 10023.

ANTHROPOSOPHICAL SOCIETY IN AMERICA

The Anthroposophical Society serves the fostering and dissemination of Anthroposophy or Spiritual Science. Its founder was Rudolf Steiner (1861–1925), scholar, educator and seer. His investigations into the world of soul and spirit are based on conscious training as described in his books, *Knowledge of Higher Worlds and Its Attainment, Stages of Higher Knowledge, Occult Science, an Outline,* and others.

Spirit research depends on organs of higher perception, and these are gradually developed in advanced stages of consciousness. The research itself depends on achievements of soul and spirit-training by which man trains his inner life to be an instrument of the same exactness as the physical instruments which aid the natural scientists of our age.

In Rudolf Steiner's books, however, the results of supersensible experiences are described in such a way that they can be studied and judged by the everyday consciousness, disciplined in the exactness and clarity of modern scientific thinking.

The Anthroposophical Society is an open society. Membership can be applied for without any pre-conditions, solely out of the recognition that such a spirit research is genuine and needed to fill the needs of our time. The work of the Society has branched out, already in Rudolf Steiner's lifetime, into many practical applications.

For further information contact: Anthroposophical Society in America, 211 Madison Avenue, New York, N.Y. 10016; (212)MU5-4618.

ARICA TRAINING

The Arica Training is a three-month residential program of physical and psychological exercises that seeks to develop what is called a Permanent 24, a level of awareness essentially beyond words and traditionally difficult to describe. However, they do say that the 24 state is a condition of total impartiality without prejudice or expectations, yet it includes those feelings of love, peace, and harmony often described as oceanic. The total environment is perceived as something precious and useful. The 24 awareness is not exotic, esoteric, or arcane. It does not belong exclusively to one cultural tradition. It is the completely natural result of a man living in the moment, and can be found in every social setting. Most people have experienced the 24 state naturally in the course of their lives, but because of the tremendous social pressure that exists for modern man these experiences are short-lived. It is possible to have this 24 awareness all the time, without leaving society, but this requires a concrete knowledge of the natural Objective Laws that govern the human psyche.

The Arica Training is designed for a global cross-cultural world; it uses the potentials of our modern society and, therefore, produces an awareness that can resist all modern pressures. It is a training of the three centers (physical, emotional, and intellectual) that harmoniously and simultaneously produce a Whole Man.

Last year several dozen Americans, ranging in age from twenty to sixty, spent ten months in Arica, Chile, studying under Oscar Ichazo, whose teachings drew upon a wide range of disciplines. These students are now the nucleus of the teaching community in New York. Mr. Ichazo oversees the teaching as it is shared with the new students.

Some of the titles of the many practices are: The Mosquito That Bites the Iron Bull, Free Mantram, The Meditation Enneagram, The Centers, Wish and Realization, Awareness During Sleep, and Tantra and Kundalini.

For further information contact Arica Institute in America Inc., 160 Central Park South, Suite 433, New York, N.Y. 10016; (212) 489–7431.

ARUNACHALA ASHRAMA

Arunachala Ashrama is dedicated to the teachings of Bhagavan Sri Ramana Maharshi, the Great Sage of modern India who taught the Path of Self-Knowledge. His central teaching is: WHO AM I?; he advises one to practice SELF-INQUIRY. THE YOGA OF WISDOM AND UNDERSTANDING taught and lived by Bhagavan Sri Ramana Maharshi is a point where East and West can meet, since it does not demand withdrawal from the world. He says, "Happiness is inherent in human beings and is not due to external causes. They must realize their *self* in order to open the store of unalloyed happiness."

Sri Arunachala Bhakta Bhagawat, a student of Bhagavan Sri Ramana Maharshi, brings his Master's teachings to those interested. There is daily chanting and meditation after which *prasad* (consecrated food) is taken and some dis-

66He alone that has
realized the Self in the
Heart has known
the Truth.**99**

RAMANA MAHARSHI

cussion is shared. Individual and group instructions are offered. A country ashram in Nova Scotia is also being formed. The New York center also has books and photographs pertaining to Ramana Maharshi.

For further information please write to Arunachala Ashrama, Bhagavan Sri Ramana Maharshi Center, Inc., 78 St. Marks Pl., New York, N.Y. 10003; (212) 477–4060.

THE ASSOCIATION FOR RESEARCH AND ENLIGHTENMENT (A.R.E.)

The Association for Research and Enlightenment is dedicated to the study and investigation of the more than fourteen thousand psychic readings given by the late Edgar Cayce, the internationally known telepathist and clairvoyant.

A.R.E. conducts a year-round program of conferences and lectures as well as a popular youth program at its Virginia Beach headquarters. The library is open to members of the Association and the general public; they are invited to research and read the Cayce material, which is thoroughly indexed.

There are more than thirteen hundred A.R.E. study groups around the world. The first group, of which Edgar Cayce was a member, was formed in 1931. This group requested and received 130 readings from Cayce while he was in a sleeplike state. From the efforts of the original group came a program and plan of activity that are the focal points of the spiritual life of A.R.E. The study groups meet weekly and try to incorporate the material from each lesson into their daily lives.

For additional information write to the Association for Research and Enlightenment, P.O. Box 595, Virginia Beach, Va. 23451; (703) 428–3588. A.R.E. also maintains a branch at 4620 E. Indian School Rd., Phoenix, Ariz. 85031. An affiliated center in New York provides lectures, workshops, seminars, conferences, study groups, and library facilities. Inquire at 34 W. 35th St., New York, N.Y. 10001; (212) 947–3885.

AWOSTING RETREAT

The Awosting Retreat studies the dynamics of body and mind, using natural methods of nutrition, activity, relaxation, and recreation that are conducive to creativity.

The Retreat is a training center for physical culture and mental and spiritual development for physiological and spiritual research.

The Retreat is located at Lake Minnewaska, New York; for information write to 315 W. 57th St., New York, N.Y. 10019; (212)765–4670.

BAHA'I CENTER

The Baha'i Center in New York holds public meetings every Sunday and also has a book sale on Friday and Saturday evenings.

For a description of the Baha'is' see page 72.

For further information contact the Baha'i Center, 25 W. 15th St., New York, N.Y. 10011; (212) 675–0171; or Susan Cox, 121 Tinker St., Woodstock, N.Y. 12498; (914) 679–9648.

BHAGAWAN SRI SATYA SAI SAMITI

The Bhagawan Sri Satya Samiti, formed with the blessings of Sai Baba himself, meets every other Friday to propagate and organize the teachings of Bhagawan Sri Satya Sai Baba, to practice Hindu rituals and bajans (holy songs), and to increase the understanding of the Hindu religion among Westerners and Indians in New York. The meetings consist of chanting, talks, meditation, and *prasad* (blessed food). There is a small library.

For further information contact Bala Sharma, 97–11 Horace Harding Expressway, Apt. 6D, Corona, Queens, N.Y. 11367.

BUDDHIST ASSOCIATION OF THE UNITED STATES

This Temple presents the teachings of Ch'an (Zen) Budhism, a meditation school, which emphasizes the direct seeing into one's original nature; the teachings of the T'ien-t'ai sect, which aims at the synthesis of existing Buddhist teachings; and Pure Land Buddhism, which teaches the faith in Amitabha Buddha (the personification of Compassion). The Reverend Log To is president.

Sunday service includes meditation, lecture, and discussion. The library is open to the public.

For more information contact the Buddhist Association of the United States, 3070 Albany Crescent, W. 231st St., Bronx, N.Y. 10463; (212) 884–9111.

BUDDHIST FELLOWSHIP OF NEW YORK

The Fellowship was founded in 1961 by eight people, all of them personal friends of the Reverend Boris Erwitt, to bring together people of non-Buddhist backgrounds to study, practice, and propagate the sublime Doctrine of the Buddha.

The bimonthly meetings of the Fellowship begin with a short service according to the ritual of the Japanese Pure Land Sect (Reverend Erwitt was ordained in Japan) and is followed by one hour or more of free discussion in which all visitors are welcome to participate.

The Fellowship publishes a small monthly bulletin called "Kanthaka," after the noble horse which bore the Prince Siddharta toward His glorious destiny. Another legendary name used by the Fellowship is "Sujata," to honor the peasant girl who saved the life of the hermit Gautama. Under the title "Project Sujata" the Fellowship practices the virtue of "Dana" (giving) by sponsoring anonymously the education of an indigent child in an American Indian reservation and providing modest scholarships for a few Buddhist students in India.

For information, contact the Buddhist Fellowship of New York, c/o Buddhist Church, 331 Riverside Dr., New York, N.Y. 10025.

CENTER FOR SPIRITUAL STUDIES

This center was founded by Rabbi Joseph Gelberman, Brother David, Swami Satchidananda, and Reverend Tai-

San in order to represent all styles of life including diverse teachings, philosophies, and theologies. In practice, the center emphasizes love in action rather than in theory. The program includes meditation, asanas, and lectures. Most of the center's activities take place in a country retreat.

For further information, contact the Secretariat, 1561 N. Benson Rd., Fairfield, Conn. 06430; (203) 259–1627.

CENTERING HOME

Centering Home is a radio program produced by Molly Scott that talks about education, spirituality, communes, organic foods, teachers, gurus, and music. Some of the people who have been on the program are Pir Vilayat Inayat Khan, Reshad Feild (a Sufi teacher from London), Sri Chinmoy, and Hilda Charlton.

Centering Home may be heard every Sunday at midnight on WRVR–FM.

CHIH JUNG T'AI CHI STUDY GROUP

To the Orientals, spirit, mind, and body are not separate but equal elements, but are seen as three aspects of one essential unity. Thus any development of mind and body must at the same time be practiced as a spiritual discipline, so that the depths of man's spirit can project spontaneously through the medium of the mind and body. The unity of mind, body, and spirit, then, does not imply bringing together separate elements but rather removing superficial mental and physical habits that prevent one from experiencing and expressing this inner unity. The Chinese philosophy of Taoism, upon which T'ai Chi is based, sees education not as an addition of something new to the individual, but as the removal of blocks that prevent the expression of one's latent potentialities that should, they feel, come forth as naturally as a stream flowing down a mountainside.

T'ai Chi Ch'uan is designed for health, vitality, longevity, and self-defense. It consists of thirty-seven different positions that are performed in continuous sequence at a slow speed without pause. Complete relaxation, accuracy of position, perfect balance, slowness and awareness of motion, and correct breathing are the elements that, when combined, help to develop the inner harmony necessary for perfect health.

The recognized inheritor of the Yang School of T'ai Chi Ch'uan is Master Cheng Man-Ching, a native of Chekiang, China, who is seventy years old. He practices and relates to Western students the living principles of an ancient civilization still alive today.

For information, write to Chih Jung T'ai Chi Study Group, 87 Bowery, New York, N.Y. 10013.

GURDJIEFF—WILLEM NYLAND

In the beginning of Gurdjieff's first series of books, *All and Everything: An Objectively Impartial Criticism of the Life of Man, or Beelzebub's Tales to His Grandson,* Gurdjieff writes about the purpose of his written work.

First Series: To destroy, mercilessly, without any compromises whatsoever, in the mentation and feelings of the reader, the beliefs and views, by centuries rooted in him, about everything existing in the world.

Second Series: To acquaint the reader with the material required for a new creation and to prove the soundness and good quality of it.

Third Series: To assist the arising, in the mentation and in the feelings of the reader, of a veritable, nonfantastic representation not of that illusory world which he now perceives, but of the world existing in reality.

Gurdjieff not only wrote about these things, he faithfully taught them through the example of his own Being.

Willem Nyland carries on the teachings of Gurdjieff, known as The Work, to groups in Seattle, Boston, Santa Fe, and Sebastopol, California.

The New York group is the main center, and information about it or any other groups may be obtained by writing to Chardavogne Barn, Chardavoyne Road, Warwick, N.Y. 10990.

G. I. GURDJIEFF

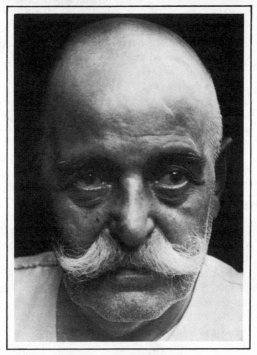

**66If you can serve a cup
of tea right,
you can do anything.ＤＤ**

HIMALAYAN INTERNATIONAL INSTITUTE OF YOGA SCIENCE & PHILOSOPHY

H. H. Sri Swami Rama is the founder and director of the Himalayan International Institute of Yoga Science & Philosophy, headquartered in Rishikesh, India. He has now established centers of this organization in Chicago, Minneapolis, and in North Salem, New York.

He held the highest position of the Hindu religion, the Gaddi or Shankaracharya of Karvirpitham, South India, which he renounced in 1952 to dedicate himself to teaching and to meditation. He studied in European universities as well as in Indian and Tibetan monasteries.

A most important part of his work to bridge Eastern wisdom and Western science has been the experiments he conducted with the Menninger Foundation in Topeka, Kansas, on voluntary control of internal states.

For more information, write to Swami Rama at P.O. Box 11283, Chicago, Ill. 60611.

IN THE SPIRIT

Paul Gorman produces a weekly "darshan on the radio," which began out of a series of tapes he broadcasted on Baba Ram Dass.

The show centers on the different kinds of sources of spiritual life, a connection between science and ecology, and the communication to people that leading a spiritual life also includes dealing with everyday problems.

Programs like the one entitled "American Spirituality," which included Whitman, Thoreau, Emerson, and Black Elk, point out that we do not have to go looking only to the East for a spiritual way of life.

"In The Spirit" can be heard every Sunday at 11 A.M. on WBAI–FM.

INTEGRAL YOGA INSTITUTE (IYI)

The Integral Yoga Institute is under the spiritual guidance of Swami Satchidananda, who gives Friday evening satsang when he is in New York.

The center offers a full schedule of daily Hatha Yoga classes; it also has classes in the scriptures, meditation, and *pranayama* (breathing).

For further information about the New York centers or any of the IYIs throughout the United States, contact the Integral Yoga Institute, 227 W. 13th St., New York, N.Y. 10014; (212) 929–0585; or 500 West End Ave., New York, N.Y. 10024; (212) 874–7500.

INTERNATIONAL CENTER FOR SELF-ANALYSIS (I.C.S.A.)

The I.C.S.A. is a yoga center for Greater Syracuse and central New York State for teaching, living, and serving in the Spirit of Yoga, unity, peace, and goodwill. It consists of an Ashram, where the art of self-analysis, self-realization and enlightened living is practiced, an Om tourist home for those coming from a distance for yogic training, and a youth center.

For further information contact I.C.S.A., 1912 S. Salina St., Syracuse, N.Y. 13205; (315) 478–8000 or 475–9142.

INTERNATIONAL DAIBOSATSU ZENDO

The newly formed International Daibosatsu Zendo, established by the New York Zen Studies Society, contains about fourteen hundred acres of land in the Catskill Mountains completely surrounded by New York State forest preservation lands.

There are buildings on the property now, but within the next two to three years, an authentic traditional Zendo will be built. A few well-trained students live here and continue daily Zazen practice and work. Each weekend about ten people from the New York Zendo come to join their retreat. At the moment, the facility is limited to members of the New York Zendo.

For more information, contact International Daibosatsu Zendo, Star Route, Livingston Manor, N.Y. 12758; (914) 439–4566.

THE INTERNATIONAL SOCIETY FOR KRISHNA CONSCIOUSNESS (ISKCON)

The International Society for Krishna Consciousness (ISKCON), often called the Hare Krishna Movement, is a cultural movement to bring peace of self to anyone. His Divine Grace A. C. Bhaktivedanta Swami Prabhupada, spiritual master and founder, has expanded the society from one small storefront on the lower East Side of Manhattan in 1966 to more than seventy branches throughout the world. These urban ashrams, or spiritual communes, are a practical demonstration of an ancient science for a modern age—a New World renaissance of Vedic culture —that includes religion, literature, drama, and art. Under the guidance of Srila Prabhupada, disciples seek to establish a style of life free from materialistic anxieties and frustrations, based on the practice of Bhaktiyoga or Krishna (God) Consciousness.

The *Bhagavad-Gita,* as it is translated and explained by Srila Prabhupada, describes Bhaktiyoga (yoga meaning connecting links with God) as the topmost yoga system, the most confidential knowledge, and the perfection of religion. It is considered simple and practical for this age because it does not require renunciation of activities but a change in consciousness. The basic principle is meditation upon the sound of the Mahamantra "Hare Krishna Hare Krishna Krishna Krishna Hare Hare, Hare Rama Hare Rama Rama Rama Hare Hare."

Festivals, feasts, lectures, and meditation are open to the public, especially on Sunday afternoons. On the East Coast the main center is 439 Henry St., Brooklyn, N.Y. 11231; (212) 596–9658; on the West Coast, 3764 Watseka Ave, Los Angeles, Calif. 90034; (213) 870–1713.

JACQUES MARCHAIS CENTER OF TIBETAN ARTS

In one of the quaintest corners of Staten Island is the property of the late Jacques Marchais. Ms. Marchais, who was in the antique business, loved Buddhist and particularly Tibetan art. She collected a great number of Asian art objects and erected a building on her property to house the pieces.

The squat quadrilateral building is in the style of a Tibetan Lamasery. One large room contains the library and the other the museum proper. Within are statues, stone Buddhas, paintings, hangings, bells, incense burners, horns, prayer wheels, and other objects relating to Tibet.

The center is open from April to October. For further information write to the Jacques Marchais Center of Tibetan Arts, 336 Lighthouse Ave., Staten Island, N.Y. 10306.

JOURNEYS TO THE CENTER

Journeys to the Center is the name Bernard and Efrem Weitzman have given to group offerings that concern themselves with the individuation process described by C. G. Jung. Through the use of fantasy, meditation, art, and movement, participants are offered the possibility of experiencing the reality of the Self and of engaging it and ego-consciousness in a dialogue essential to the process of becoming whole. Both Bernard and Efrem Weitzman are psychotherapists.

For further information write to or call Journeys to the Center, 251 W. 95th St., New York, N.Y 10025; (212) 362–3700.

KUNDALINI YOGA CLASSES

Tim Kapeluck, a student of Yogi Bhajan, gives basic classes in Kundalini Yoga on Monday, Wednesday, and Friday at the Guild of Craftsmen on Tinker Street.

For information, write to Tim Kapeluck, 5 Rock City Rd., Woodstock, N.Y. 12498.

THE LITTLE SYNAGOGUE—THE MIDWAY COUNSELING CENTER

This is a modern Hassidic congregation that is dedicated to the joyful pursuit of meaning and purpose in a challenging world.

The Little Synagogue is indeed small in structure, although its followers number in the thousands. Its philosophical origin was conceived with the deliberate theme of keeping it small and personal. It embraces the idea that a house of spiritual encounter must provide an oasis and retreat from the materialism and impersonal communication in most areas of urban living today.

It believes that the aspect of denominations—such as orthodox, conservative, and reformed—can create a denial in the character of true spirituality. It uses, therefore, a universal approach with the essence of the traditional approach of Judaism. Its emphasis is on a new Hassidic approach that seeks personal growth and "joy through worship." It is dedicated to the commitment that only through joy can we encounter the God dwelling within us. Some of the activities of the Little Synagogue include The Wisdom Academy, which sponsors "Wisdom Wednesdays," an adventure in life enhancement; lectures and classes in the Kabbalah, and the Wisdom Press, which publishes booklets on religion, psychiatry, metaphysics, and Kabbalah.

Rabbi Joseph H. Gelberman is the founder of the Little Synagogue and director of the Midway Counseling Center. He also founded the Metaphysical Circle and the Wisdom Academy.

The Midway Counseling Center specializes in individual, group, and family therapy. It is dedicated to the client who suffers estrangement, feelings of isolation, insecurity, and disintegration of personal effectiveness. By joining the disciplines of religion and psychotherapy, the center hopes to serve the troubled and unaffiliated in the search for personal and spiritual wholeness.

Rabbi Gelberman also conducts summer seminars on the terrace of his home, and has an open house there on every national holiday. Once a year there is an evening called "The Swami and the Rabbi" with Rabbi Gelberman and Swami Satchidananda.

For further information about either of these organizations, contact: The Little Synagogue, 27 E. 20th St., New York, N.Y. 10003; (212) GRamercy 5–7081 or 866–3795.

MONICA LOVETT—YOGA

Classes are held to calm, revitalize, and release your integral energy through Yoga, bio-energy, voice-vibrations, movement, sensory awareness, and meditation. Results from these energy-releasing methods show that people have achieved not only physical reconditioning, but also great empathy within themselves and others.

For further information contact Monica Lovett, 122 E. 91st St., New York, N.Y. 10028; (212) 348–7369 or PLaza 7–6300.

LUCIS TRUST

The world activities of the Lucis Trust are dedicated to establishing right human relations. They promote the education of the human mind toward the recognition and practice of the spiritual principles and values upon which a stable and interdependent world society may be based. The Lucis Trust is nonpolitical and nonsectarian.

The Arcane School was created by Alice A. Bailey in 1923 as an adult training school in meditation techniques and the development of spiritual potentiality. The school provides sequential courses of study and meditation and practical training in group service. The Arcane School is conducted by correspondence through headquarters in New York, London, Geneva, and Buenos Aires at no charge.

The Lucis Publishing Companies. The Lucis Publishing Company of New York and the Lucis Press Ltd. of London publish the books of Alice A. Bailey.

The *Beacon* magazine is published bimonthly by the Lucis Press. This is a magazine of esoteric philosophy presenting the principles of the Ageless Wisdom teaching as a contemporary way of life.

Triangles is an activity of the mind, using the power of thought and of prayer to invoke light and goodwill for all mankind. The work is done by units of three people who link each day in thought for a few minutes of creative meditation. They need not necessarily live in the same locality, and many "international" triangles exist.

World Goodwill action at present consists of the distribution of literature all over the world in many languages; it cooperates with the UN and its specialized agencies. It publishes a newsletter and commentary and provides a study course on the fundamental problems of humanity.

Full Moon Meditation Meetings ,are held in the Exhibition Hall (2nd floor), Carnegie Endowment International Center, United Nations Plaza at 345 East 46th Street, New York City. These meetings use group meditation as an act of cooperation with the Plan of Hierarchy for humanity.

The Lucis Trust Library is open to everyone—in person or by mail—Monday through Friday.

For further information contact Lucis Trust, 866 United Nations Plaza, Suite 566–7, New York, N.Y 10017; (212) 421–1577.

MACROBIOTICS

Macrobiotics is a simple, natural manner of living. A diet of grains and vegetables is eaten, supplemented by a variety of other foods as well as personal preferences.

Macrobiotics allows one to regain and maintain his health and sensitivity. The quiet preparation and consumption of whole, natural foods can create a certain peace and tranquility for thinking, reflecting, and generally appreciating the world around and within us.

For information about lectures, massage, and cooking classes, contact Miss Shizuko Yamamoto, 23 W. 73rd St., New York, N.Y. 10023; (212) 877–7807; or Bob Feldman, c/o Eder, Apt. 15D, 910 West End Ave., New York, N.Y. 10025; (212) 865–3407.

MACROCOSMIC STUDY HOUSE

The Macrocosmic Study House has twelve people living and working together who are interested in macrobiotics, massage, yoga, meditation, astrology, and palmistry. There are informal discussions and lessons on macrobiotic cook-

ing and food. They also have a lending library of macrobiotic literature.

For more information call the Macrocosmic Study
House, 390 Pacific St., Brooklyn, N.Y. 11217; (212)
875–8547.

MATAGIRI

Matagiri is a center devoted to the realization of the
spiritual teachings of Sri Aurobindo and the Mother; it
distributes books written by and about Sri Aurobindo and
the Mother and provides information on the Sri Aurobindo
Ashram and Auroville, the universal city now being built
in India as a manifestation of the new consciousness envisioned by Sri Aurobindo.

For information contact Matagiri, Mount Tremper, N.Y.
12457.

MEDITATION

"The individual can reach the Godhead with the help of
any one of the millions of ways of worshiping the Form
and the Formless. He could go to a temple or pray at home.
He could pray while walking, standing, sitting or even re-
clining. But he must pray. He may sing bhajans, hear discourses or just relax and meditate. He may take recourse to
any one of the different types of yoga suitable to his
physical and mental set up. . . . In the ultimate analysis
the Form (saguna) and the Formless (nirguna) are one,
and unless one realizes this unity in diversity one is prone
to become fanatic—and this should be avoided at all costs."
—SWAMI MUKTANANDA

At the weekly meditation evening devotees of Swami
Muktananda meditate, chant bhajans, and read from his
writings. Occasionally a tape is heard or films of the ashram
in India are shown.

If you are interested in learning more of the activities
of Swami Muktananda and his devotees write to Studio
Rear Building, 502 E. 84th St., New York, N.Y. 10028.

MEDITATION

Meditation and instruction as taught by Louise Berlé explores "The Nature of Reality and The Creative Principle," combining the essence of both Eastern and Western concepts of universal truth. With a background in Western metaphysics, Japanese Zen Buddhism, and Indian Vedanta, Ms. Berlé's teaching is based mainly upon her mystical experiences and revelations of cosmic structure and process. Emphasis is upon the expansion of awareness, love, and the determination of personal circumstances. The group meets every Tuesday and Friday evening.

For further information contact: Louise Berlé, 41 W. 57th St., New York, N.Y. 10019; (212) PLaza 5–6250.

MEDITATION

Hilda Charlton spent eighteen years in the East and studied under many great yogis. She holds group meditations, teaching the works of the Masters, especially Sri Sathya Sai Baba, every Friday evening.

For information phone (212) 866–5328 between 12 and 2 P.M.

MEHER BABA CENTER

Readings and discussions of Meher Baba and other sages are held.

Address all inquiries to Tom and Yvonne Riley, 381 Joy Rd., Woodstock, N.Y. 12498; (914) 679–7138.

MEHER BABA HOUSE

Meher Baba House is open to everyone, and includes a library, photographs, and books for sale. Throughout the week the House has activities that include films, talks, meditations, and readings from the *Discourses*.

For more details contact Meher Baba House, 186 W. 4th St., New York, N.Y. 10014; (212) 989–9527.

SWAMI MUKTANANDA

❝Kneel to your own Self.
Honor and worship your own
Being.
Chant the mantra always
going on within you.
Meditate on your own Self.
God dwells within you as you.❞

MEHER SPIRITUAL CENTER

The Meher Spiritual Center, Inc., located north of Myrtle Beach, South Carolina, is dedicated to Meher Baba, who visited there on three occasions. It was located in 1944 and developed for a retreat in anticipation of his coming from India with his disciples from the East and joined by his many followers from the West. When asked who could come to the Center after his last visit, Meher Baba replied, "Those who love and follow me and those who know of me and want to know more."

For information about visiting, write to Meher Spiritual Center, P.O. Box 487, Myrtle Beach, S.C. 29577; (803) 272–5295.

V. R. MUNSIFF, INDIAN ASTROLOGER

V. R. Munsiff learned astrology in his native country, India, and has been doing charts for over thirty years. He feels that this system of Hindu astrology casts more light for the individual than does Western astrology. He also teaches Hindi, the national language of India.

For further information write to V. R. Munsiff, 3530 Rochambeau Ave., Apt. 5A, Bronx, N.Y. 10467.

THE NEW AGE CENTER FOR ESOTERIC STUDIES, INC.

The New Age Center for Esoteric Studies is under the direction of Pir Vilayat Inayat Khan, an adept of an Order of Sufis of the East, who is also the head of similar schools in London and Paris.

The Center functions as a universal school for the study of inner truths in all religions and esoteric schools. It seeks to bring about spiritual renewal and to encourage understanding and brotherly affection between all persons.

Practical instruction in the various forms of meditation developed by the religions and esoteric schools of the world is held. There are lectures and discussions on various religious teachings as they concern meditation, prayer, and

HILDA CHARLTON

❝See the divine spark in
everybody and everything;
then your separateness
ceases, you become one
with the light shining
in every living thing.❞

essential truths in sutras, mantrams, sacred texts, and esoteric symbology. Congresses are addressed by the representatives of the major religions of the world, with participants engaging in lectures and discussions of their respective religious teachings from a world point of view. There are also interfaith religious services, shared activities with other groups with similar goals, and seminars and workshops for the development of students along spiritual lines.

For further information contact Charlotte Leblanc, 157 E. 72nd St., New York, N.Y. 10021.

NEW YORK THEOSOPHICAL SOCIETY

The New York Theosophical Society offers study groups in theosophy, H. P. Blavatsky's *Secret Doctrine,* astrology, and symbology, and meditation workshops and lectures on these and related subjects. There is also a library open to the public.

The Quest Bookshop publishes books on meditation, astrology, Buddhism, yoga, parapsychology, and other New Age subjects. They also sell books on these subjects published by others.

For further information contact the New York Theosophical Society, 242 E. 53rd St., New York, N.Y. 10022; (212) 758–5521.

NEW YORK ZENDO OF THE ZEN STUDIES SOCIETY, INC.

Shobo-ji, "The Temple of the True Dharma," is the name that its Abbot, Soen Nakagawa Roshi, gave the New York Zendo to express its aspiration and to encourage its students to incorporate Dharma teachings into every aspect of their lives.

New York Zendo-Shobo-ji was founded and is directed by the Reverend Eldo Tai Shimano (known as Tai-San) for the purpose of fostering the Bodhisattva spirit in the lives of its students by means of the Rinzai Zen method of training in Mahayana Buddhism.

The term "Bodhisattva spirit" means a spirit of real love and compassion for sentient beings, from a grain of dust to all our fellow beings, animate and inanimate. A true Bodhisattva resolves to give himself and all that he is and has, not only during his life, but also during all the lives to come.

The empathy and compassion of the Bodhisattva are developed through continual spiritual purification, the cultivation of a deep sense of responsibility, and, most importantly, through self-discipline. The central and indispensable element in Zen Buddhist discipline is daily Zazen practice.

"Zazen" is a Japanese term consisting of two characters: za, "To sit (cross-legged)," and zen, from the Sanskrit "dhyana," which is at once concentration, dynamic stillness, and contemplation. Zazen is a method of training mind and body together. Correct sitting posture and correct breathing help to quiet the mind and focus psychic energy and thus to strengthen dhyana. With time and with sincere effort in Zazen practice, mind and body, inside and outside, self and other become one. This condition of Zazen is known as Samadhi.

As the Zen student continues in his practice, loneliness, dissatisfaction, and the sense of the meaninglessness of modern life vanish in the marvelous clarity of Samadhi. No longer searching externally for answers, the student journeys inwardly to reach the moving spirit of the Buddha, his own self-nature. He becomes alive, more creative, and is filled with Bodhisattva, longing to share his great joy with all his fellow beings.

Through devotion and persistence, the aims of Zazen are eventually realized. The first is Enlightenment. With this experience, Samadhi is fulfilled; mind and body, the self, and the universe are seen to have been, from the beginning, one Reality. The second and more difficult aim of Zazen is the actualization of the Bodhisattva ideal in every moment of daily life.

As usually understood, Zen refers to a particular Buddhist school, but in broad terms, Zen is not just Buddhism. The essence of Zen is the experience of truth that is at the heart of all religion, art, and culture. Through its universality, Zen may offer the best hope for mankind.

The Sangha meets for Zazen several times a week in the mornings and evenings. The meetings consist of two or three Zazen periods of forty to fifty minutes, alternating with ten-minute *kinhin*, wailing Zazen. Sutras are chanted during each meeting. Students may consult individually with the director on a regular basis about their Zazen practice.

At Shobo-ji, a year is divided into two training periods of approximately five and a half months each. The Zendo is completely closed for several weeks in June and December between training periods.

Days of special significance in the traditions of Zen Buddhism are observed by formal services and chanting, as are times of particular meaning to the Sangha.

A two-day retreat, or *sesshin*, is held at the Zendo once a month. Students rise at 4:30 A.M. and spend the entire day in Zazen practice. While doing formal Zazen, while chanting, listening to lectures, walking, eating, cleaning the Zendo, even while sleeping, the student must continue his individual Zazen practice and be constantly mindful and aware. To foster concentration, strict silence is observed. The sesshin leader provides encouragement and guidance with a daily lecture ("teisho") and daily private interviews ("dokusan") with each student.

Several times a year, sesshin is expanded to prove seven days of training. A week of continuous, single-minded Zazen in a disciplined and supportive atmosphere improves each student's practice and provides an opportunity for spiritual growth. Because of limited space and the importance of prior training, sesshin participation is limited to members of the Sangha.

There are three classes of students in the Sangha: regular students, out-of-town students, and students whose responsibilities limit them to infrequent participation.

Thursday evening Zazen meetings are open to the public. Group instructions in Zazen, Zazen practice, and a lecture are given, followed by one of two periods of Zazen in the Zendo.

The Zen Studies Society, Inc., a nonprofit corporation consisting of a seven-member board, owns the Shobo-ji Zen Temple property at 223 East 67th Street, and offers it to the New York Zendo Sangha for Zazen practice. Besides an authentic Zendo (meditation hall), the building includes a Zen garden and Japanese rooms that help to create a tranquil atmosphere.

Soen Nakagawa Roshi, Abbot of Shobo-ji and Daibosatsu Zendo and of Ryutaku-ji in Mishima, Japan, is the successor to the modern giant Zen master, Gempo Roshi, and is one of the few English-speaking roshis in the world. His students, many of whom are Westerners, have helped to establish sanghas in Los Angeles, Honolulu, London, Cairo, and Jerusalem. Soen Roshi spends most of the year in Japan and New York, visiting the other groups when time allows.

Reverend Shimano is president of the Zen Studies Society, and director of the New York and Daibosatsu Zendos. In 1960, after a long period of training under Soen Roshi, Reverend Shimano was sent by his teacher to the West. He worked with a Zen group in Hawaii until 1965, when he settled in New York City. He founded the New York Zendo in 1968.

Although he has completed the traditional koan training, Reverend Shimano does not use the title "Roshi." Traditionally, to assure true Dharma succession, a Zen teacher did not assume this title until he had attained a spiritual maturity equal to or surpassing that of his own teacher. Reverend Shimano wished to revive this practice, out of concern for transmission of the Dharma.

For more information contact the Zen Studies Society, 223 E. 67th St., New York, N.Y. 10021.

NICHIREN SOSHU OF AMERICA

For a description see California entry page 112. In New York, there are study meetings on Wednesday, Thursday, and Friday evenings at the Riverside Plaza Hotel, 2nd floor, on West 73rd Street between Broadway and West End avenues.

Individual meetings are held throughout the city. For information call Mr. Sudo, Nichiren Soshu of America, 250 W. 57th St., Room 521, New York, N.Y. 10019; (212) 246–2215.

NOUMEDIA

The Noumedia tape catalog is filled with listings on New Age subjects of human growth, humanistic psychology, and conscious awakening. The speakers on these tapes talk about the social-cultural-spiritual upheavals going on around us that are a manifestation of the evolution of man. A major theme of these tapes is the vivification and unification of modern knowledge so that the heart of man is awakened as well as his head.

The Noumedia library is addressed to laymen as well as to all those in the helping professions, whether student or practitioner.

A few of the speakers you can hear on these tapes are Baba Ram Dass, Frederick S. Perls, William C. Shutz, Chogyam Trangpa Rinpoche, Margaret Mead, Ronald D. Laing, Pir Vilayat Inayat Khan, Ira Progoff, and Haridas Chauduri.

HARI OM

COMMUNICATION IN PEACE

For information contact George Fisher, Noumedia Co., Box 750, Port Chester, N.Y. 10573.

CHARLES PONCE—SEMINARS ON THE I CHING

Charles Ponce is the founder and director of AZOTH: The Foundation for Archetypal Studies. He is the author of *The Nature of the I Ching: Its Usage and Interpretation; The Kabbalah Today: A Student's Handbook;* and *The Skeptic's Guide to the Occult Sciences.* Mr. Ponce has lectured and conducted seminars on the I Ching and related topics at leading universities, colleges, and organizations throughout the United States.

For information about his New York seminars, write to
W. B. Agency, 551 Fifth Ave., New York, N.Y. 10017.

RADHA SOAMI

Lectures and discussions on the teachings of Master Charan
Singh Maharaj Ji are held at the George Washington Hotel
at least twice each month. These Satsangs also include
chanting and meditation.

For further information contact the New York Radha
Soami Society, George Washington Hotel, Lexington Ave.
at 23rd St., New York, N.Y 10010; or William J. Grimaldi,
9511 Shore Rd., Brooklyn, N.Y. 11209; (121) 23–1422.

There are thirty-nine Radha Soami centers throughout
the country. For information about the center closest to
you, write to H. F. Weekley, 4600 Connecticut Ave.,
#309, Washington, D.C. 20008.

RAMAKRISHNA-VIVEKANANDA CENTER OF
NEW YORK

Swami Nikhilananda is the head of the New York Rama-
krishna-Vivekananda Center.

See page 131 for a description of Ramakrishna-Vive-
kananda.

For information about the New York center, write 17
E. 94th St., New York, N.Y. 10028.

RAM DASS SATSANG

This is an open meditation basically founded on Ram
Dass's teachings as can be found in his book *Be Here Now*
and in tapes of his talks. The purpose is to be together in
satsang. From time to time there are tapes and slides.

Meditation and satsang are held on Wednesday and
Friday evening.

For more information call (212) 252–6289.

RUHANI SATSANG (The Path of the Masters)

The Masters have taught that we were placed in life to know ourselves and to know God. They tell us, by their own perfect experience of the way, that we are of the same essence as that of God, born in His image, and that, although we have become lost in the duality and separateness of the senses and have led ourselves further and further away from what we truly are, into confusion and suffering, we have the birthright to know the unspeakable effulgence of God existing within us. The Path of the Masters gives us the contact with our birthright; it opens our inner eye and ear to the experience of the soul; it leads us to the knowledge of the Self and, ultimately, of God.

There are certain instructions by which the living Master Kirpal Singh wishes every prospective initiate to abide before he gives initiation. He must cultivate and develop noninjury to all living creatures, truthfulness, the life of chastity, love for all living creatures and more so for all human beings, and selfless service to all living creatures. He must also practice the purities of diet, livelihood, and conduct.

It is a path of love, discipline and self control. After the initial spiritual experience given at the time of Initiation, the rest depends on relentless regular practice as enjoined by the Master.

Every speaker after God is enjoined to maintain a strictly impartial record of his daily conduct, so as to find out his weaknesses and try to weed them out one by one. This diary is to be sent to the Master every four months for further guidance.

The New York Group of Ruhani Satsang has a public satsang every Sunday. There is a one hour meditation preceding it for initiates only. The Satsang is held at 33 West 14th Street.

All of the Kirpal Singh groups have a literature table containing free literature and books for sale.

Other groups in the New York Area are: Lower Manhattan Satsang, 2 Washington Square North; Doris Yokelson, Quaker Bridge Road East, RFD Box 317, Croton-on-

❝The human mind is the throne of God.❞

KIRPAL SINGH

Hudson, N.Y. 10520; (914) 271–9762; Mrs. Ruth Seader, 8 Copper Beech Pl., Merrick N.Y. 11566; (516) 378–6183; Kirpal Ashram, Worcester, Vt. 05682.

For information on other centers throughout the country contact the national representative, T. S. Khanna, 11404 Lakin Pl., Oakton, Va. 22124.

RYOANJI TEMPLE STONE GARDEN

A replica of the 500-year-old Ryoanji Stone Garden (the Zen Garden in Kyoto, Japan) and Hill-and-Pond Garden is at the Brooklyn Botanical Gardens, which are open from April 1 to October 31, weather permitting. Phone in advance: (212) 622–4433.

SANT BANI ASHRAM—KIRPAL SINGH

Sant Bani Ashram, located outside of Franklin, New Hampshire, was founded by the great living Master Kirpal Singh on October 11, 1963, during his second American tour.

It serves as a retreat and center for meditation and study for initiates of the living Master and for those seekers after Truth who are drawn to him and wish to learn more. Initiates are encouraged to come for brief, intensive stays ranging from a few days to two weeks, to work on their meditation and to practice Surat Shabd Yoga as taught by the Master.

Since the Master teaches that every initiate must earn his own living and perform his duties and obligations in the world, this program of intensive meditation is intended for refreshing and recharging, and not as a permanent way of life for any initiate.

Sant Bani Ashram is one of two ashrams in the Western world dedicated to the living Master Kirpal Singh Ji and following this program; the other is Kirpal Ashram, Worcester, Vermont. (There are, of course, many in India, including the Master's headquarters, Sawan Ashram in Delhi.)

It serves as a center and headquarters for the work in New Hampshire of presenting the teachings of the Master, giving initiation, and so on. For this purpose, a public meeting is held Sunday at 1 P.M., classes are conducted for people desiring initiation. In this aspect, the Ashram is one of perhaps seventy-five centers in the Western world devoted to the propagation of the Master's teachings (administrative headquarters are in Oakton, Virginia, and Anaheim, California). The Master has about 90,000 disciples in all, the great majority of whom are in India.

It further serves as a publication and distribution center for many of the Master's books, and for his monthly magazine, *Sat Sandesh.*

At the present time there are four family groups living at the Ashram (each in his own home) plus two or three others, who are there to work and assist in all of the above activities. They all have regular jobs in addition to serving at the Ashram. While greater agricultural self-sufficiency is definitely a goal, the Ashram is not a commune or community; and the number of permanent residents, at the Master's specific request, is kept low—just enough to do the necessary work.

For more information write Sant Bani Ashram, Franklin, New Hampshire.

SATYAM SHIVAM SUNDARAM—(I AM TRUTH, I AM GOD, I AM BEAUTY)

Satyam Shivan Sundaram Ashram is basically a yoga laboratory where experiments are conducted that involve man's psychic energy. Anxiety is released through various forms of yoga practice guided by Shyam Bhatnagar, a student of Harish Johari, a Naada yogi. Mr. Bhatnagar also advises students privately in Princeton and in New York about psychic centers in the body and how to regulate energy for their spiritual growth.

For information write to or call Satyam Shivam Sundaram, 425 Alexander St., Princeton, N.J. 08540; (609) 924–4883.

SELF-REALIZATION FELLOWSHIP

Meditations and services are held on Thursday evenings and on Sunday mornings from 10–12 noon at the Hotel Biltmore, Madison Avenue at 43rd Street.

For a further description of SRF see page 118.

SENSORY AWARENESS—CHARLOTTE SELVER

Sensory Awareness is the name originally given by Charlotte Selver to a study based on the teaching of Elsa Gindler of Berlin, which Ms. Selver brought to the United States in 1938. Her many students, including Frederick Perls (who incorporated it into his Gestalt therapy), a number of New York psychologists, and numerous figures associated with Esalen Institute, have spread this work throughout the country.

The depth and purity of the work has not always been maintained, for it is a discipline that can easily be distorted into superficial sensationalism. In the European original, as well as in Ms. Selver's version of it, Sensory Awareness is the patient and sustained study of sensing, i.e., the undisturbed conscious function of the sensory nervous system in the total environment, through an endless variety of simple experiments. Any activity can be used, provided it is used for its own sake as experience, not to achieve a preconceived end.

The whole difficulty of the discipline is that it goes against all our usual forms of training, which have definite objectives, while it might be said of Sensory Awareness that its objective is to have no objective—not even spontaneity or fun, to take an extreme example—but rather to arrive at an openness for whatever unanticipated sensory messages may come. It is no training, in any literal sense, but an intuitive unfolding of innate capabilities, bringing an openness to inner and outer experience, and a deeper relating to what one does.

Ms. Selver and her husband, Charles Brooks, who for many years conducted the work with her, maintain a studio at 160 West 73rd Street in New York City. They have a Western address at Big Sur, California, and give annual spring workshops at the Zen monastery in Tassajara. During the summer, they work in Monhegan, Maine, and during the winter in Mexico.

SENSORY AWARENESS—CLYDEEN MALLOCH

From our social conditioning, we have learned to put a screen between ourselves and the world. Through simple, nonverbal experiments, you can learn to experience more fully such everyday things as sitting, standing, walking, and playing.

Clydeen Malloch worked with Dr. E. C. Whitmont and Betty Keane in an experimental group combining Jungian analysis and Sensory Awareness. She studied with Charlotte Selver and Charles Brooks in their classes in Sensory Awareness for five years.

For further information, contact Clydeen Malloch, 15 Dean St., Brooklyn, N.Y. 11201; (212) 852–0538.

SENSORY AWARENESS—ALICE SMITH

Alice Smith teaches Sensory Awareness in the Selver-Brooks New York studio during the spring term and leads weekend seminars at the studio and elsewhere.

For twelve years she has studied and trained with Charlotte Selver and Charles Brooks in this work, which originated with Elsa Gindler in Germany fifty years ago. Our quiet way of exploring how we sit, stand, move, and touch can lead to a stronger sense of self and a new freedom to participate in our daily activities and relationships.

For further information, contact Alice Smith, 223 E. 66th St., New York, N.Y. 10021.

SENSORY AWARENESS—EFREM WEITZMAN

Sensory Awareness is about life itself. It asks us to trust who and what we are again and to unbind the knots with which we have met the blows and demands of the cultural and emotional environment that surrounded our formative years and that are with us still. We believe that in every aspect of our daily being and doing lies the possibility and opportunity for renewal, for freeing, for realizing the potential that we know this life in us promises.

Efrem Weitzman is a disciple of Charlotte Selver and has taught for four years at growth centers, universities, and hospitals as well as at his own studio. Call (212) 362–3700 or 749–6571 for information concerning classes.

SENSORY AWARENESS AND NONVERBAL COMMUNICATION

Sensory Awareness is a physical reorientation based on the way a person experiences himself. It is a process of self-discovery to help us become more aware of how we may unconsciously restrict and interfere with our natural organismic tendencies toward balance, renewal, and relaxation through exploring to what degree we cooperate or interfere with the natural needs of the organism. Since the sense organs are the means through which we perceive reality, many psychiatrists have found it a useful aid to therapy. However, the work also stands on its own. The student becomes his own teacher through a more total awareness of how he functions and his repeated personal experience that something within him really has the understanding of what he needs to function more fully.

Ms. Keane teaches at the New School for Social Research, 66 W. 12th St., New York City. She also works with private pupils and groups and is a co-therapist with Dr. Edward C. Whitmont in group psychotherapy in her studio. For more information write to 470 West End Ave., New York, N.Y. 10024.

SHAKTI PARWHA ASHRAM (3HO)

The 3HO Foundation stands for the Happy, Healthy, Holy way of life that Yogi Bhajan has helped to establish in seventy-two centers across the country.

Kundalini Yoga is the Yoga of Awareness. Yogi Bhajan's method includes the disciplines of Hatha, Raja,

Laya, and Bhakti Yogas. The purpose of this teaching is not to gain disciples, but to train teachers who are vessels of the Holy Name.

For further information contact Shakti Parwha Ashram, 610 Manor Rd., Staten Island, N.Y. 10314.

SHREE GURUDEV RUDRANANDA YOGASHRAM

The basic purpose of yoga is to achieve freedom, happiness, and enlightenment that has nothing to do with mind, emotions, or a structured system. It has to do with the organic structure of a human being nourished by the love of God manifested through his detachment of all material things. By taking from all manifestations the content, we come to the true realization of our nothingness while being in the world. The only thing to surrender is attachment. Joy and the sense of growth either exist every day or there can never be an ultimate realization. Through our daily realization we can see the pattern of our ultimate realization. Reality is today and realization is tomorrow.

Teaching at the Shree Gurudev Rudrananda Yogashram is based on principals of yoga, primarily Kundalini Yoga. All spiritual work can be served because the teaching doesn't exclude anything. The classes are not open to the general public.

For an interview write to or call Shree Gurudev Rudrananda Yogashram, 88 E. 10th St., New York, N.Y. 10003; (212) 254–0670 or 929–8054.

Other centers around the country are: Gregg Brodsky, Lost Clove Rd., Big Indian, N.Y. 12410; (914) 254–9807; Shree Gurudev Ashram, 609 N. Locust St., Denton, Tex. 76201; (817) 382–9354; Michael Shoemaker, 312 W. 14th St., Bloomington, Ind. 47401; (812) 338–3215; Dr. John Mann, State University College, Department of Psychology, Geneseo, N.Y. 14454; (716) 245–5115; ZBS Media, R.D. #1, Fort Edward, N.Y. 12828; (518) 695–6406.

SIVANANDA CAMP-RETREAT-POCONOS

Sivananda Camp–Retreat–Poconos is a simply run Ashram adapted to Western needs that follows the example of the late Swami Sivananda. The retreat is under the guidance of Swami Lakshmy Devi, its basic practice being "Serve, Love, Meditate, Realize." The basic yoga discipline, "No Smoking, No Meat, No Sex, No Drugs," is followed here. The Ashram is opened to guests year round.

For information write to Sivananda Camp–Retreat–Poconos, R.D. 3, Stroudsburg, Pa. 18360.

SIVANANDA YOGA VEDANTA CENTER

The Sivananda Yoga Vedanta Center of New York was formed by Swami Vishnu-devananda in 1958 to promote the realistic understanding of yoga and to practice its basic teachings.

Swami Vishnu-devananda is a close disciple of the renowned Saint and Yogi H. H. Sri Swami Sivananda Maharaj, who founded the Divine Life Society and Yoga Vedanta Forest Academy in Rishikesh, Himalaya.

The New York Center is run by Swami Ramananda, a student of Swami Vishnu. At the New York center, special attention is given to classes in yogic postures, breathing, and relaxation. These classes are held daily by Swami Ramananda and other instructors, all personally trained by Swami Vishnu. For students interested in the spiritual aspect of yoga, regular meditation is held daily in addition to a meditation class with readings from the *Bhagavad-Gita* on Wednesday nights and courses in meditation and Vedanta philosophy for beginners on Friday nights. On Sunday nights, staff and students have a prayer meeting.

From time to time, weekend retreats are organized at a country location providing a welcome opportunity for students of other centers to meet and exchange views with the New Yorkers.

Interest among the New York students in pure yogic

vegetarian cooking is promoted by meals served after the evening classes.

The staff of the center consists of voluntary workers who wish to progress spiritually on the path of yoga and simultaneously to serve humanity through selfless work. Under the guidance of Swami Ramananda, the staff is also being trained to take over the direction of another branch either already existing or to be established.

There are nine Sivananda Yoga Vedanta centers throughout the United States and Canada. For information regarding the branch nearest you or for additional information contact Sivananda Yoga Vedanta Center, 243 W. 24th St., New York, N.Y. 10011; (212) ALgonquin 5–4560.

SOCIETY FOR AVATAR MEHER BABA

Meetings and discourse classes at the Society's headquarters are held weekly for those who are enrolled; meetings for the general public are held once a month. There are at least two large public celebrations a year held under the auspices of the Society.

For further information contact the Society for Avatar Meher Baba, 121 W. 72nd St., New York, N.Y. 10023; (212) 799–4850.

SPIRITUAL REGENERATION MOVEMENT

Maharishi Mahesh Yogi is a spiritual teacher from the Himalayas who has come to teach a simple system of meditation to all who wish to learn it, so that they may come daily to that state of pure Being or transcendental consciousness that has been described in the West as the Kingdom of Heaven within. With this daily experience, the nature of Being gradually infuses into the ordinary mind so that in time the mind remains illuminated by its light under all circumstances.

For many years, Maharishi has traveled throughout the world, teaching this method to householders of many countries; wherever he has been he has left a center of the

Spiritual Regeneration Movement to carry on his work. He was a disciple of Swami Brahmananda Saraswati Maharaj, Shankaracharya of Jyotir-math.

Transcendental meditation is natural and effortless, and starts to be effective from the beginning. Introductory talks on the basis and background of Maharishi's teaching are given.

For additional information please call or write to Spiritual Regeneration Movement, 277 West End Ave. New York, N.Y. 10023; (212) 362–1070.

SRI CHINMOY

Thousands of spiritual seekers throughout the world have found their paths to inner fulfillment illumined by the radiance of Sri Chinmoy's unparalleled realization. Dedicated aspirants are drawn in increasing numbers to the Sri Chinmoy centers, which have expanded to a total of seventeen in eleven countries in the past seven years. Still more people have joined the campus meditation groups established at the universities visited by the Master during several extensive lecture tours. Sri Chinmoy is the only Eastern spiritual figure to give meditations at the United Nations.

There are many Sri Chinmoy centers throughout the United States. For information regarding them, contact Sri Chinmoy Centre, 85–45 149th St., Jamaica Hills, N.Y. 11435.

SRI CHINMOY BLACK MEDITATION

It is understood that we the Black Disciples and followers of Sri Chinmoy, are interested in pursuing a higher course in life, a life of the soul. Our spiritual life is based on a belief in a Supreme Being and the value of service to all peoples (in particular, to the black people). As such, we disavow the use of drugs, alcohol and nicotine, in attaining our goal in life.

We also feel that as disciples and followers of Sri Chinmoy, being recipients of his Light, Peace and Power,

SRI CHINMOY

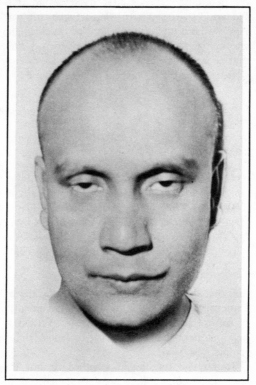

❝O Supreme, to Thee I offer
What I am: my life's
soulful gratitude.
O children of the Supreme,
to you I give what I have:
my life of dedicated
service and oneness.❞

we have a unique and significantly dynamic role to play in our world today. We offer ourselves to our people and the world as examples of what spiritual life can accomplish. And we hold the lofty standard of the Supreme as a joyous alternative to the life of despair, sorrow and dissipation, that so many of our brothers and sisters experience.

Ours is the life of Peace, Joy, and Divine Fulfilment.

We offer our souls, in service,
AUM SHANTI

For further information call Prabuddha (212) 989–5719.

SUFI DANCING

TOWARD THE ONE, THE PERFECTION OF LOVE, HARMONY AND BEAUTY. THE ONLY BEING, UNITED WITH ALL THE ILLUMINATED SOULS WHO FORM THE EMBODIMENT OF THE MASTER, THE SPIRIT OF GUIDANCE.

Spiritual dancing is that which elevates the consciousness. Dancing may be said to be the movement of the body or any of its parts to rhythm; the spiritual is that which helps to make man realize that his body is really the divine temple.

It may be questioned whether or not these are folk dances. Of course, they are folk dances. There have been groups like Dervishes, and even Shaking Quakers, who use dance forms. The Bible has much to say about this, and traditional religion, little. The development of ecstasy has always been regarded as beneficial to the young to help them rise above the denseness of the earth.

These dances came through Sufi Ahmed Chisti, a Sufi Murshid (guide). In New York, dancing occurs at least twice a week.

For information write to or call Shahabu-d-din, 551 Hudson St., Apt. #9, New York, N.Y. 10014; (212) 741–0927.

SUFI ORDER

For any information in the Woodstock area regarding the Sufi Order established in the West by Hazrat Pir-O-Murshid Inayat Khan, his writings, related material, and information about Pir Vilayat Inayat Khan, contact Jean (Fatha) Miller by phoning (914) 679–6015 or 679–8333.

T'AI CHI CH'UAN

Courses at the Asian Martial Arts Studio are given in T'ai Chi Ch'uan, Kung Fu, and karate. These courses are designed to teach the students to relate to themselves physically and mentally as one, to attain spiritual awareness, and for self-defense.

All the arts are taught in the classic form stressing Zen Meditation. Their most popular course is T'ai Chi Ch'uan, where the emphasis is on relaxation, breathing, and sensitive movements.

For additional information write to, phone, or visit the Asian Martial Arts Studio, Richard Chin, director, 5 Great Jones St., New York, N.Y. 10003; (212) 255–1904 or 475–1116.

T'AI CHI CH'UAN

T'ai Chi Ch'uan is an ancient Chinese system for activating the body in order to attain physical, mental, and emotional harmony. The essential quality is the way of moving. It is slow, even, light, continuous, and in balance, each form flowing into the next without stopping, in a long composition of 108 forms.

Sofia Delza is a dancer who has lived in China where she studied T'ai Chi Ch'uan with the eminent Master Ma Yueh-Liang. She has also studied the Dance-Art of the classical Chinese theatre.

For information about classes contact Sofia Delza, Chelsea Hotel, 222 W. 23rd St., New York, N.Y. 10011; (212) 243–3700.

T'AI CHI SOCIETY OF NEW YORK

The *I Ching,* or *Book of Changes,* represents one of the first efforts of the human mind to place itself in the universe. It has exerted a living influence in China for three thousand years. First set down in the dawn of history as a book of oracles, the *Book of Changes* deepened in meaning when ethical values were attached to the oracular pronouncements; it became a book of wisdom, eventually one of the Five Classics of Confucianism, and provided the common source for both Confucianist and Taoist philosophy.

Professor Da Liu, a Chinese philosopher and Master of T'ai Chi Chu'an (Chinese exercise), proposes the teaching of *I Ching* as a book enabling man to explore the cosmic truth and thus fulfill human nature. This approach to the mystery of life also provides the serious student with the means to foretell the course of his own destiny, thus enabling him to choose his own path with knowledge and foresight.

For information about T'ai Chi or *I Ching* classes, contact the T'ai Chi Society of New York, 310 E. 42nd St., New York, N.Y. 10017; (212) 661–8030.

TAIL OF THE TIGER (Buddhist Meditation Centers)

Chogyam Trungpa Rinpoche, born in Tibet in 1939, received the highest ordinations in Mahayana and Tantrayana Buddhism—Kargyupa-Nymapa lineage. He left Tibet in 1959 because of the Communist invasion and went to India where he taught at the Young Lama's School. With the blessings of H. H. the Dalai Lama and H. H. Karma he went to England in 1964 to study at Oxford University, where he studied comparative religion and Western culture. In 1967 he established his first teaching and meditation center, Samye-Ling in Eskdalemuir, Scotland. In 1970 he came to the United States and has subsequently founded two major centers and several smaller centers in major cities.

The purpose of the centers is to provide a highly intense

situation of meditation, not only sitting practice, but also the meditative approach to daily life, or learning how to dance with chaos, to transform negative energies. The centers are set up as communities with a certain number of permanent members; new ones are accepted all the time, and there are constant visitors, who stay from a day to several months. Everyone at a center is expected to participate in the daily life—house chores, farming, craft center—as well as the three one-hour meditations and the ten-hour sessions on Wednesday at the Tail and Sundays at Karma Dzong. There are also mountain retreat huts for completely isolated retreats.

Several intensive seminars are given each year by Rinpoche on the various aspects of meditation, Tibetan Buddhism, and the Buddhist texts.

They also publish a magazine called *Garuda* twice yearly.

There are meditation groups working under Rinpoche's direction in New York, Boston, Montreal, Toronto, San Francisco, Los Angeles, and Burlington, Vermont. Anyone interested should contact Tail of the Tiger, Star Route, Barnet, Vt. 05821; (802) 633–9389; or Karma Dzong, Salina Star Route, Boulder, Colo. 80302; (303) 447–2693.

TEMPLE OF UNDERSTANDING

The Temple of Understanding Inc., is an educational, non-profit, tax-exempt organization designed to increase public understanding of the great world religions, including Buddhism, Christianity, Confucianism, Hinduism, Islam, and Judaism.

The organization's major undertakings have included the world's first Spiritual Summit Conference held in Calcutta in 1968, and the second Spiritual Summit Conference held in Geneva in 1970.

As a significant part of its programs, the organization proposes to construct a Temple of Understanding that will be a symbol of understanding among the religions and a world center of education about them.

For more information write to Temple of Understanding,

Finley P. Dunne, Jr., Executive Director, 1346 Connecticut Ave., N.W., Washington, D.C. 20036.

UNITED LODGE OF THEOSOPHISTS

Theosophy, or the Wisdom Religion, is a complete body of knowledge that has existed from time immemorial. Its knowers are the Elder Brothers of humanity—the Buddhas and Christs—whose periodic efforts to enlighten the race constitute the eternal Theosophical Movement. The present theosophical movement wishes to form the nucleus of a universal Brotherhood of Humanity, without distinction of race, creed, sex, caste, or color; to study comparatively the world's religions, sciences, and philosophies; and to investigate the unexplained laws of nature and the psychical powers latent in man.

Theosophy's chief tenets are the Deity as an impersonal divine principle inherent in all life; individual immortality, since each man is a spark of that one flame; Karma, the law of cause and effect; reincarnation, and cycles. The goal of all human striving, reached through repeated incarnations upon earth, is Buddhahood or Christhood, called by some philosophers "the realization of the SELF," which is the meaning of true Yoga.

As an informal association of students of Theosophy, the United Lodge of Theosophists is sympathetic to all sincere efforts to free men's minds from the shackles of outworn creeds. In its own efforts, however, it points to the writings of H. P. Blavatsky and William Q. Judge as constituting the authentic message of Theosophy for this age. These writings, it holds, are the most effective means for pushing forward the work of liberation, and for providing at the same time the guiding principles for the new age Man.

U.L.T. centers exist in Los Angeles, San Francisco, New York, Philadelphia, Washington, other American cities, and Canada, as well as in foreign lands.

For further information contact United Lodge of Theosophists, 347 E. 72nd St., New York, N.Y. 10021; (212) 535–2230

VEDANTA SOCIETY OF NEW YORK

For a description of Vedanta see page 131.

For information about the Vedanta Society of New York write to Swami Pavitrananda, 34 W. 71st St., New York, N.Y. 10023; (212) TRafalgar 4–8691.

YOGA AND ASTROLOGY

Tom McKee teaches yoga and astrology at Ulster County Community College for the Centre of Continuing Education in Stone Ridge, New York. His interpretation of the horoscope emphasizes the Spiritual Potentiality of individuals and helps them to be aware of their problems so that they can consciously overcome them. Yoga and astrology classes are also held in Kingston, New York.

For information contact: Tom McKee, R.D. 6, Box 76, Kingston, N.Y. 12401; (914) 338–7808.

YOGA FOR LIFE

Rahila Devi is Yoga Instructor for the Department of Continuing Education of the State University of New York at New Paltz. She offers two yogas: the Hatha and Rajah Yoga Course geared more toward the physical aspects of yoga, with the stress on keener awareness and experiencing the body as a temple of the Spirit, and the Meditation and Philosophy Course, which includes Rajah Yoga techniques of Concentration and Meditation not included in the Hatha Yoga Course. Her courses include the study of Sound and Light Energy with an emphasis on Mantra Yoga. She also teaches these courses in Kingston, New York.

Another course taught in her home is one on diet where students make whole-wheat bread, chapattis, and some Indian vegetarian dishes, learn about the use of spices, and learn how to make yogurt, sprout beans, and some macrobiotic dishes.

Originally from Calcutta, India, Rahila Devi met her Guru, Dr. Rammurti Mishra, in New York City and studied with him for several years. She studied with Dr.

Haridas Chaudhuri in San Francisco at the California Institute of Asian Studies, and with Sant Keshavadas, the Indian Kirtanist.

For further information contact Rahila Devi, R.D. #6, Box 76, Sawkill Rd., Kingston, N.Y. 12401; (914) 338–7808.

YOGA SEMINARY OF NEW YORK, INC.

The Yoga Seminary of New York, Inc., also known as the Bhakti-Jnana Yoga Ashram, is a branch of the Divine Life Society. In 1969, Swami Chidananda performed a puja to officially open the ashram.

The main activities are weekend retreats that consist of meditations, chanting, yoga, and Gita classes.

For further information contact Sita Frenkel, Yoga Seminary of New York, Inc., P.O. Box 421, Harriman, N.Y. 10926; (914) 783–1842.

YOGA THERAPY CENTRE

The Yoga Therapy Centre specializes in training beginners in Hatha Yoga. Emphasis is on therapeutic yoga breathing with all movements, postures, relaxation techniques geared to encourage the individual to learn how to "tune in" to his or her own psyche and get away from "just doing calisthenics." Meditation courses are offered regularly and weekend programs are available.

For further information contact Yoga Therapy Centre, 36 W. 26th St., New York, N.Y. 10010; (212) 741–0722.

YOGI GUPTA ASSOCIATION

The method used at the Yogi Gupta centers is usually individual, carefully conceived by Yogi Gupta to produce maximum results in minimum time.

The center offers classes in posture, breathing, concentration and relaxation, psychic development, food concepts, and philosophy. For information regarding class participation, lectures, demonstrations, contact Yogi Gupta Association, 127 E. 56th St., New York, N.Y. 10022; (212) 759–1548.

YORE—YOGA ORGANIZATION FOR RESEARCH AND EDUCATION

YORE is a nonprofit organization that is engaged in training Yoga teachers, developing study materials for teachers and for students' home study, and doing research on the ways that Yoga may aid special groups such as senior citizens, the mentally ill, children, alcoholics, and drug abusers.

Besides classes in Hatha Yoga for the groups mentioned, teachers conduct classes in Hatha and Raja Yoga in many New Jersey towns and in the Philadelphia area. They also give lectures, seminars, weekend workshops, and retreats, and counsel small study groups. Members receive a quarterly paper and are invited to monthly Sat-Sangas, informal gatherings for discussions with a leader or teacher.

Katherine Da Silva is founder-president of YORE.

For further information write to YORE, P.O. Box 471, Rutherford, N.J. 07070.

ZEN MEDITATION CENTER OF ROCHESTER

Philip Kapleau spent thirteen years disciplining himself in Zen Buddhism in Japan under three masters before being ordained a Zen teacher by Yasutani-Roshi in 1964.

Shortly after the publication of his first book, *The Three Pillars of Zen* (1966), Mr. Kapleau came to Rochester to found the Zen Center. In addition to conducting monthly sesshins (Zen seclusions), giving private instruction, writing, and offering guidance in all areas of Center activity, Mr. Kapleau conducts workshops on Zen at universities and growth centers throughout the country.

For further information contact the Zen Meditation Center of Rochester, 7 Arnold Park, Rochester, N.Y. 14607; (716) 473–9180.

BOSTON
AND VICINITY

ANANDA MARGA ASHRAM

This center is founded on the teachings of Sri Ananda-murati, the guru of "the path of bliss." Its emphasis is on the Ananda Marga meditations, which are derived from the original Tantric Yoga of Shiva. The group's work stresses a dual emphasis on individual meditation and social service.

Activities include Asana classes, Dharma Shakra class, Philosophy class, and a Sunday songfest and meditation.

This center is the headquarters for the Ananda Marga Ashrams on the East Coast.

For further information contact Ananda Marga Ashram, 63 Wendell Street, Cambridge, Mass. 02138; (617) 491–3691 or 491–3646.

THE ASHRAM

The Ashram is the central agency of an extensive integral yoga teaching organization that offers classes all over New England. The center gives classes in teacher training, including courses in hatha, raja, and bhakti yogas and anatomy, under the auspices of the Ashram Yoga Teacher's Association, founded in 1965.

In addition, the Ashram sponsors yoga retreats, with instruction in hatha, raja, bhakti yogas and meditation techniques, in Lancaster, Massachusetts.

For further information phone Joann Sherwood at (617) 599–2939.

ASTROLOGY, MEDITATION, PLUS—LOUIS ACKER

Louis Acker possesses the increasingly valuable combination of Eastern and Western knowledge. He is both a scientist and an occult philosopher, and out of the two has originated and researched scientific theories on the nature of psychic forces.

He is also teacher in the New England School of Astrology as well as a yoga and meditation instructor.

For further information contact: Louis Acker, 548 Pleasant St., Belmont, Mass. 02178; (617) 484–4802.

ASTROLOGY—CHARTS AND READINGS

Abraham Sussman draws up astrological charts and offers readings in which he stresses actually experiencing the energies of the planets. He demonstrates and teaches this through astrological walks, breath patterns, and other unusual practices.

For further information contact Abraham Sussman, 145 Aspinwall Ave., Brookline, Mass. 02146; (617) 734–7947.

ASTROLOGY—ISABEL HICKEY

Isabel Hickey is one of the spiritual *mamajiis* (mothers) of Boston. She is an astrologer with a full schedule of readings, astrology classes, speaking, and media engagements.

She leads an informal discussion and meditation group every Friday evening at Hyppocrates Health Institute, 25 Exeter Street, Boston. She also holds astrology classes there on Monday evenings.

For further information phone (617) 923–9387.

BAHA'I FAITH

The Baha'i faith follows the teachings of Baha'Ul Allah, a proclaimed prophet who lived from 1817 to 1892 and whose primary work was to further the message of global unity. According to the Baha'i tradition, it is by renewing the spiritual aspects of man that practical and worldly problems can and will be solved.

Practices include daily prayers in conjunction with physical movements, and frequent feasts. All practices are aimed toward "the unfettered search after truth," one of the basic tenets of the teachings of Baha'Ul Allah.

Classes are held weekday evenings in both Cambridge and Boston.

For information call (617) 536–8511

EAST-WEST YOGA CENTER

This center, one of the oldest yoga and meditation institutes in the Boston area, sprouted from the Hatha Yoga classes of Patricia Harvey Shelton, one of the directors of East-West.

The center has grown to include a city ashram house in Boston, a wide variety of classes, and a center for visiting teachers of many schools of yoga.

Hatha-Raja yoga sessions are held for both adults and children. Over twenty classes are taught each week, including instruction in prisons, hospitals, schools, and colleges. All Hatha classes include a great deal of meditation, with usually at least half the class time spent on it.

The center provides ten-week teacher training programs in Hatha Yoga and meditation.

Tibetan and Sanskrit language classes are taught by Arthur Mendelbaum, with attention paid to the spiritual foundations of these languages.

Daily meditations are held. The evening meditation offers instruction in Tibetan Yoga techniques of the Kargupa sect and in accordance with the teachings of Trumgpa Rinpoche, spiritual guide of the ashram.

For further information contact the East-West Yoga Center, 105 Marlborough St., Boston, Mass. 02116; (617) 267–8056.

HARE KRISHNA CENTER (ISKON)

The Boston devotees of the Hare Krishna movement, under the spiritual guidance of Swami Bhaktivedanta, can often be seen in Harvard Square or on the Boston Commons chanting the name of God. The group here is active and insistent in encouraging concentration on the divine through prayer and chanting. They follow the Hindu tradition of devotion, Bhakti Yoga, in every aspect of their lives, including dress and eating habits.

Members of the center live together in a large house in Allston, where they offer Sunday feasts, chanting, transcendental plays, and readings from the *Bhagavad-Gita* or *Sri Isopanisad*.

For further information contact the Hare Krishna Temple, 40 N. Beacon St., Allston, Mass. 02134; (617) 782–8892.

HATHA YOGA—LAURA CENESI, JACK LINK

Laura Cenesi and Jack Link offer beginners weekly Hatha Yoga classes at Old Cambridge Baptist Church, 1151 Massachusetts Avenue, Cambridge, Massachusetts.

HATHA YOGA—MARGO LaBORDE

Margo Laborde teaches daily yoga classes at Hyppocrates Health Institute, utilizing the integration of breathing with postures. She emphasizes small classes and individual attention; her goal is to open the self physically, mentally, and emotionally to higher energies and forces.

For further information contact Hyppocrates Health Institute, 25 Exeter St., Boston, Mass. 02116; (617) 267–4183.

HATHA YOGA—JOHN LODER

John Loder has been teaching Cambridge's largest and oldest Hatha Yoga classes for over five years. The classes, which usually number well over 150 people each, are consistently rhythmical and balanced, with asana and breath work followed by relaxation and meditation.

Mr. Yoder, an environmental architect, sees the classes as an opportunity to realize continuously the path of Karma Yoga, devotional duty to God in the world.

All are welcome to attend at the First Parish Unitarian Church, 3 Church St., Cambridge, Mass. 02138.

HATHA YOGA—JOEL ZIMMERMAN

Joel Zimmerman offers a unique Hatha Yoga experience that combines asanas (postures) with music, chanting, and massage. Weekly classes are presently held on Thursdays at St. Peter's Episcopal Church in Central Square, Cambridge.

For further information contact Joel Zimmerman, 63 Wendell St., Cambridge, Mass. 02138; (617) 491–3691.

HYPPOCRATES HEALTH INSTITUTE

Dr. Ann Wigmore, founder and director of the Hyppocrates Health Institute, maintains that "the body is the holy temple in which He dwells" and that "we are needed by the Almighty." "It is through it that He can carry out His many plans" and "if we abide by Nature's laws, health and youth are ours."

Based on this understanding, as well as many years of inner and outer research, she has created a healing center that draws young people concerned with purifying their bodies and living organically and older people seeking to renew failing health.

The Institute prescribes a diet of pure, organic, raw fruits and vegetables, as well as offering a regimen of fasting and cleansing. In addition to lectures on health, nutrition, and ecology, the center offers classes in massage, reflexology, Hatha Yoga, and astrology.

For further information contact Hyppocrates Health Institute, 25 Exeter St., Boston, Mass. 02116; (617) 267–4183.

KARMU

Karmu, sometimes known as Edgar Warner, car mechanic, is a unique part of the Boston-Cambridge spiritual circuit. His tiny disheveled apartment on Green Street, Cambridge is crammed nightly with an assortment of people that defies description. Some come depressed and down; Karmu feeds them, talks to them, loves them, and they do get better.

Karmu reigns every evening from about 7 to midnight, and all day Sunday. The hours and the scene are informal and always unpredictable, but all are welcome anytime;

Karmu, 526 Green St., Cambridge, Mass. 02139; (617) 354–6970.

KUNDALINI YOGA

Kundalini Yoga, as taught by students and devotees of Yogi Bhajan, has its Boston area center in Lexington. Beginning and intermediate classes are taught twice weekly in both Boston and Cambridge. Advanced classes are held once a week in Lexington.

Kundalini Yoga is, according to David Lee, head of the Boston Center, "a powerful and positive method to lead us to realize who and what we are." As it is a method, the student actively participates in powerful breathing exercises, specific Kundalini Yoga kriyas and meditations. As one begins to study this method one releases the body tensions and clears the mind so that the true nature of the person shines forth brightly.

For further information contact David Lee, Guru Ram Dass Ashram, 21 Robbins Rd, Lexington, Mass. 02173; (617) 861–8714.

MACROBIOTICS

The large and active macrobiotic community of Boston is augmented by the presence of Misho Kushi, a wise and learned authority of the macrobiotic philosophy of Yin and Yang, a system that encompasses everything from metaphysics to food and family life.

Mr. Kushi lectures every Tuesday and Thursday evening at the Arlington Street Church, on the corner of Boylston and Arlington streets in Boston.

In addition, there are a number of macrobiotic houses in both Boston and Cambridge, some of which offer macro cooking classes. For information about these classes phone (617) 734–3853.

The Tao Bookstore at 303 Newbury Street in Boston, and the East West Journal together act as connection centers for the macrobiotic community. Contact either for further information.

MEHER BABA CENTER

Cambridge–Boston Meher Baba devotees hold weekly meetings every Thursday evening. The gatherings are offered as worship to Baba, and include readings from his works and a short meditation. The Baba Information Center is open from 4 to 9 P.M. Monday through Saturday.

For further information contact Meher Baba Information Center, 7 Inman Sq., Cambridge, Mass. 02139; (617) 491–9637.

NECTAR—THE NEW ENGLAND CENTER FOR THERAPY AND REBIRTH

NECTAR is a unique experiment both in combining communal living and the establishment of an extensive and carefully developed social institute and in combining the Eastern and Western worlds.

The center offers a series of day-long "Integrative Intensives," which combine the methods of Western humanistic psychology and Eastern spiritual teachings. These experiences include primal scream therapy, meditation, dervish dancing, Gestalt games, and Zen relating exercises. The group also runs weekly groups in primal and Gestalt therapies.

This work is a significant step toward integrating the "spiritual" world with the reality of the individual being, and to bridge the gap between "the spiritual and the profane."

The group is one of those involved in Satsang.

For further information contact NECTAR, 145 Aspinwall Ave., Brookline, Mass. 02146; (617) 734–7947.

THE NEW ENGLAND SCHOOL OF ASTROLOGY

The New England School of Astrology is a learning center founded and directed by Frances Sakoian, astrologer, healer, and spiritual counselor with forty-four years of experience. Ms. Sakoian travels and lectures all over New England, appears on television and radio, runs encounter

workshops, gives personal astrology readings and acts as
director of the American Federation of Astrologers. She
has published *The Complete Astrology Guide,* or "The
Encounter with the Self."

The Astrology School offers a full set of courses on
astrology, as well as studies in spiritual healing, physical
therapy, and meditation.

For further information contact Frances Sakoian, 1
Monadnock Rd., Arlington, Mass. 02174; (617) 648–
5578.

NICHIREN SHOSHU OF AMERICA, BOSTON KAIKAN

The Nichiren Shoshu school of Buddhism seeks the state
of total harmony of all aspects of existence. Its means to
this end is the Experience of the harmony of body and
mind, self and environment, physicality and spirituality primarily through the repetition of the ancient sutric phrase
"nam myoho renge kyo."

The emphasis is on life in and of the world, "devoted
to happiness, the essence of Buddhism." Happiness is "the
attainment of enlightenment through perfection and the
realization of *all* desires."

The center has introductory meetings four times a week.
Singing, chanting the lotus sutra, talking, questions and
answers, guidance from Mr. Kubo, head of the New
England General Chapter of Nichiren Shoshu.

For further information contact Nichiren Shoshu of
America, Boston Kaikan, 82 Charles St., Boston, Mass.
02114; (617) 723–6420.

RAMAKRISHNA VEDANTA SOCIETY

Swami Sarvagatananda is in charge of the Boston Vedanta
Center and leads services each Sunday in which meditation
is coupled with the explanations of the principles of
Vedanta and other religions and the readings from Ramakrishna. Swami also gives classes on the *Bhagavad-Gita*
and speaks at the chapel at Massachusetts Institute of
Technology weekly.

SARADA DEVI

❝As a wind removes the clouds,
so the name of God destroys
the cloud of worldliness.❞

The Society has a retreat, Sarada Ashrama, in Marshfield, Massachusetts, which is active in the summer months as a center for a "life of meditation, prayer, and other spiritual practices," as well as classes on the scriptures and daily spiritual instruction by Swami Sarvagatananda and other visiting Swamis.

The Boston Center includes a small, well-stocked bookstore with selections on religion, philosophy, and psychology.

For further information contact The Ramakrishna Vedanta Society, 58 Deerfield St., Boston, Mass. 02215; (617) 536–5320.

RUHANI SATSANG—KIRPAL SINGH

There are nightly meditations at the home of Ted Hastings, a disciple of Master Kirpal Singh (see page 48 for description). Meditations on Sunday are at the Harvard Divinity School (new building).

For further information about Ruhani Satsang in the Boston–Cambridge area, contact Ted Hastings, 50–52 Irving St., Cambridge, Mass. 02138; (617) 868–8399.

SATSANG

This is an unusually open and eclectic group experiment in integrated and ever-changing *satsang,* "the coming together of seekers on the spiritual path." It is a New Age venture open to all teachings and forms of meditation, ritual, practices, music that work. Satsang is the central communal gathering for the various Cambridge seekers circuit and ascertains the unity of this large family.

Meetings are held on Monday evenings at the Episcopal Theological Seminary, Tyler Reading Room, 99 Brattle Street, Cambridge, Massachusetts.

For further information contact Ron White or Jonathan Leif, 145 Aspinwall Ave., Brookline, Mass. 02146; (617) 734–7947.

SIDDARTHA FOUNDATION FOR THE STUDY OF HIGHER CONSCIOUSNESS

The Siddartha Foundation is a multichanneled endeavor seeking to "research and examine the spiritual roots of man as a living force." Its members, ranging from university physicists to parapsychologists, share a sense of urgency about the need in this Age of familiarizing Man with a knowledge of spiritual law and universal consciousness. Toward this end they are working on a number of projects, both in research and communications.

Among these projects is a proposed television series that will present in-depth studies of some of the most highly evolved loving persons. According to Richard Turner, director of the Foundation, "In all parts of the globe our cameras will study these exceptional human beings in the very places which have nurtured their spirituality. We will study their beliefs, their ceremonies, and most importantly the inner strengths and powers manifested through them. As much as is humanly possible, by showing these and the very steps of their development, we can enable our viewers who are ready to actually experience the higher consciousness of these individuals."

A second Foundation project involves aiding in the preservation of a rare collection of Tibetan books and manuscripts, threatened by damp-climate deterioration since their removal from the Tibetan Buddhist Monastery of Thyangboche, Tibet, to Nepal, India. A member of the Foundation, through the aid of a Ford Foundation grant, is presently setting up a microfilming project to record the collection. Further funding is being sought to produce a television special covering this work.

Siddartha Foundation also sponsors centering seminars, concentrated sessions "to help people understand that at the very core of their beings they already know the answers to the most important questions in their lives." The two-day programs give participants the ability to reach high levels of consciousness. Emphasis is placed on universal laws, consciousness projection and dream technology.

For further information contact J. Richard Turner, 91 Dobbins St., Waltham, Mass. 02154; (617) 899–2356.

SIVANANDA YOGA CENTER

This yoga and meditation teaching center offers various forms of instruction. Emphasizing the universality of spiritual teachings, it introduces six classical types of meditation, leaving each student free to choose his own path. Methods are taught both formally and informally, and integration of methods is stressed.

Formal classes include daily open asana (Hatha Yoga) classes; a six-week course in Hatha Yoga, including breathing exercises and lectures; a six-week meditation course, teaching the six classic methods; and a Sunday evening satsang consisting of chanting and group discussions and sitar concerts with Shambhu Das, disciple of Ravi Shankar.

For more information contact Sivananda Yoga Center, 16 Hamilton Rd., Apt. 3, Brookline, Mass. 02146; (617) 734–1726.

SRI AUROBINDO CENTER

The yoga of Sri Aurobindo, Hindu Master, emphasizes completing the circuit of the rise to higher consciousness with the descension of this consciousness to the material world, where mind, life, and body are transformed and Oneness realized.

Aurobindo's final word is that "we are, whether we like it or not, 'members one of another.' Unless we realize this truth, and act upon it, we shall never have peace and goodwill on earth."

Eugine Finn, an Aurobindo devotee, offers private instruction in the teachings of Sri Aurobindo and The Mother. The work includes some Hatha Yoga as well as other meditation practices.

For further information contact Eugine Finn, 91 Kilmarnok St., Boston, Mass. 02215; (617) 262–6390.

STUDENTS INTERNATIONAL MEDITATION SOCIETY

SIMS, the Boston-Cambridge branch of Transcendental Meditation, follows the teachings of Maharishi Mahesh Yogi and offers introductory lectures every Wednesday and Thursday evening. In addition, the Center is open daily to all TM students.

For further information contact Students International Meditation Society, 27 Concord Ave., Cambridge, Mass. 02138; (617) 876–4581.

SUFI DANCING

Sufi dancing combines chanting, mudra movement, and music in a New Age form of meditation. It is based on esoteric laws and teachings of the Sufi Masters, but with an emphasis on nonattachment to forms of the past. The first experience is *joy,* a central theme in the Sufi tradition.

From that point, the dances ascend in many directions, all with the emphasis on making spiritual truths an experienced reality. There are dance walks of the planets and of the divine attributes as well as dances utilizing sacred phrases of all the major religions of the world. More advanced Sufi work includes breath and sound meditation.

The dancing is based primarily on the inspiration of Murshid Samuel Lewis and the teachings of Pir Vilayat Khan, disciples of Hazrat Pir-O-Murshid Inayat Khan.

For more information contact Muniera Morgan, 70 Concord Ave., Somerville, Mass. 02143.

SOTGO—SERVERS OF THE GREAT ONES

The Servers of the Great Ones is a nonprofit organization, absolutely apolitical, presenting through the growing influences of its members an image that will keep with the highest principles of Mankind, embracing all, regardless of origin, race, nationality, creed, religion, sex, or social standard. It will provide the necessary means to implant the standards, disciplines, and teachings of the Great

Ones to all those who will strive for the Supremacy of the Spirit and who are in agreement toward the establishment of a World Peace. It will encourage by precept and example the movement toward a spiritual reeducation for Humanity adhering to the teachings of the Great Ones within a Group Consciousness of a Universal Scope.

Public meditations are held every Wednesday evening, based on "impersonal service to humanity."

For more information contact SOTGO, 48 Beacon St., Waltham, Mass. 02154.

TAI CHI

Master Liang describes the Yang Style of Tai Chi that he teaches as a "meditation in action and action in meditation, based on ancient Chinese classical dance used for health and self-defense." He is available daily for individual instruction as well as for a number of class periods weekly.

All classes are held at 77 Gainsborough Street, Apt. 1F, Boston.

For further information contact Master Liang, (617) 262–7037.

CALIFORNIA
AND VICINITY

AJA-PA—BREATH METHOD

The Ajapa-Breath Method is the most ancient method of breathing. Its origin can be traced in almost all Sanskrit books: Vedas, Upanishads, and Samhitas. It was called Atma-Vidya (science of Self) and Brahma-Vidya (science of the Absolute).

In ancient times it was taught to everyone by the Guru-disciple method, but became almost lost in time. In our time only a few teachers know about this method and of these only Guru Janardan Paramanhansa, affectionately known as Guruji, at the instruction of his own Guru during a vision, is disseminating it to everyone. He is on a mission prophesied by his Guru to prove the enormous power of the Ajapa-Breath Method to the modern scientific world.

The Ajapa-Breath Method is the outcome of research conducted by the Rishis (wise men) in ancient times to understand man and his relationship to the universe. The purpose of human life in the world is to know this relationship exactly and practically. It is claimed by the Rishis that by knowing this, one can know everything.

The Ajapa-Breath Method is not an exercise with imposed conditions. It can be done all the time like normal breathing and is unbelievably simple.

A trained initiator of Guru Janardan Paranhansa alone can impart this instruction which takes twenty to thirty minutes. After the instruction, the initiator and the North American Center keep in touch with the individual through correspondence and give further guidance when necessary.

For further information contact Branch Center, Ajapa-Breath Method, 6446 W. Olympic Blvd., Los Angeles, Calif. 90048. Other centers are: Branch Center, Ajapa-Breath Method, 514 Waukegan Rd., Glenview, Ill. 60025; and North American Center, Ajapa-Breath Foundation, 4801 Draper Ave., Montreal 253, Que., Can.; (514) 486–2844.

ANANDA MARGA YOGA SOCIETY

Ananda Marga feels that every individual's goal in life should be to realize God. This supreme realization comes as a result of experiencing all things in the universe as manifestations of one Cosmic Consciousness.

In order to realize this goal Ananda Marga teaches that a person must practice meditation, which allows one to put himself into a more harmonious relationship with the universe. In its system of meditation Ananda Marga uses mantras, which are subtle sound vibrations that produce mental expansion and elevation when repeated mentally or orally.

Ananda Marga (Path of Eternal Bliss) was founded in 1954 by the great Master of Yoga, Shrii Anandamurtiji. The universal mantra given by Anandamurtiji for all the world to sing is: *Baba Nam Kevalam.*

The director of Ananda Marga in the U.S. is Acharya Yatiishvarananda Avadhuta (known as Dadajii, which means respected brother). Dadajii is one of a thousand disciples of Shrii Anandamurtijii who have been responsible for carrying the Master's teachings to millions of people in India and elsewhere.

If you would like more information, write to their national headquarters at 3453 E. 12th St., Wichita, Kans. 67208. Ananda Marga Centers are located in every state. On the West Coast Ananda Marga, P.O. Box D, Stanford, Calif. 94305; on the East Coast write to Ananda Marga, 64 Wendell St., Cambridge, Mass. 02138.

ANANDA MEDITATION RETREAT

Geodesic domes sit like giant crystals on a hilltop that was pushed up through the earth's crust some thirty millions years ago. Truth-seekers sit in ancient postures and listen to teachings of a five-thousand-year-old science as interpreted by Paramahansa Yogananda, a great modern Master of Yoga. A blender whirs, and a tiny lizard scuttles for safety. The new and the old join hands in a dance of eternity.

Ananda Meditation Retreat was founded in 1967 by Swami Kriyananda. After nearly twenty years of teaching yoga (Kriyananda became a direct disciple of Yogananda in 1948), he purchased some land, partly for a personal seclusion, partly to give others a chance also for personal spiritual renewal. Now some twenty residents and visitors from around the world join him in his quest. Like all of Kriyananda's work, Ananda is dedicated to Paramahansa Yogananda and his line of gurus.

Meals are vegetarian and, as much as possible, organic. Most of the vegetables served come from their own gardens. Because the meals are an integral part of the atmosphere, and a natural opportunity for visitors to talk with residents, they encourage all retreatants to "break bread" with them.

Each week the Saturday classes place special emphasis on a different path of yoga. Classes are given in raja (meditation), hatha (postures), karma (service), and bhakti (devotion). There is also a free-form weekend each month with classes on subjects closelv related to yoga, such as spiritual astrology, diet and cooking, cooperative communities, and natural medicine.

For additional information write to Ananda Meditation Retreat, Allegheny Star Route, Nevada City, Calif. 95959; (916) 292–8958.

ANDERSON RESEARCH FOUNDATION, INC.

The Anderson Research Foundation is a nonprofit corporation dedicated to research in Life Enhancement. Recognizing that no one way is the only way, the foundation takes an eclectic stance. It sponsors research in the emotional, physical, mental, spiritual, philosophical, religious, nutritional, and other approaches to life enhancement, both accepted and unaccepted. Dr. Lawrence Anderson is the director.

For more information contact Anderson Research Foundation, Inc., 3968 Ingraham St., Los Angeles, Calif. 90005; (213) 387–9164.

THE AQUARIAN ORACLE

The Aquarian Oracle is interested in any style of life, any philosophy or technique that brings more joy and happiness, greater satisfaction, self-awareness, and fulfillment.

The Oracle will be a New Age organic life project, the work goal of a cooperative religious group popularly known as the Oracle people.

For additional information, write to the Aquarian Oracle/Relative, P.O. Box 29293, Los Angeles, Calif. 90029.

ARCANA

Arcana is a group meditation training center that tries to relate spiritual goals to community needs. They consider the highest human creative capacity to be the genius to solve major urgent community problems and they attempt to relate newly acquired knowledge and newly developed skills to the general welfare. Individual growth and talent that remain unrelated to community need merely add to the karmic burden of humanity. Their's is an attempt to ease some of that burden.

For further information write to or phone Arcana Workshops, 407 N. Maple Dr., Suite 214, Beverly Hills, Calif. 90210; (213) 273–5949 or 374–8389.

BAHA'I FAITH

The Baha'i Faith is a world religion based on three onenesses, or Unity: the oneness or unity of God, the unity of His Manifestations (the Major Prophets), and the essential or underlying unity of all major religions. The goal of the Baha'is is a world civilization based on the laws of God brought by Baha'u'llah, its founder. The principle of the Oneness of Mankind is the pivot around which all the teachings revolve.

For information contact the Baha'i Faith, 2219 Derby St., Berkeley, Calif. 94505; (415) 845–8249.

THE BARKSDALE FOUNDATION

The Barksdale Foundation—For Furtherance of Human Understanding—is a nonprofit organization engaged in disseminating information on how to achieve more harmonious and rewarding interpersonal relationships and a more creative and productive life; it sponsors seminars, encounter groups, and workshops for this purpose. The foundation also maintains a free lending library of over a thousand volumes on psychology, philosophy, sociology, anthropology, religion, metaphysics, self-discovery, E.S.P., and related subjects. The founder and director of the foundation is L. S. Barksdale.

For additional material write to The Barksdale Foundation, Suite 223, Crenshaw Sq., 3860 Crenshaw Blvd., Los Angeles, Calif. 90008.

BERKELEY ZEN CENTER

The Berkeley Zen Center practices zazen to express their true nature and to be at one with the source of all things. Its priest is Mel Weitsman. Berkeley Zen Center is affiliated with San Francisco Zen Center, which is headed by Richard Baker, the successor to Suzuki Roshi, Zen Master.

For information contact the Berkeley Zen Center, 1670 Dwight Way, Berkeley, Calif. 94703; (415) 845–2403.

BLUE MOUNTAIN CENTER OF MEDITATION

It is the aim of the Blue Mountain Center of Meditation to bring the ancient Hindu art of meditation into the midst of daily life by adapting it to the needs and environment of modern man.

Spiritual values of a universal nature are translated into everyday practice with the aid of meditation to enable the individual to release and harness his deeper resources for the welfare of those around him; to solve his own personal problems, improving family and community relationships; and to fulfill the Supreme Goal of life by realizing God within his own consciousness.

Everyone is encouraged to make meditation the basis of daily life within his own religious and cultural environment.

Eknath Easwaran comes from an ancient Hindu family of Kerala State, South India. He looks upon his mother's mother as his spiritual teacher. She taught him by her saintly life that the Supreme Goal of life is to know God and become united with Him.

Classes in meditation, conducted by Eknath Easwaran, consist of reading and commentary on the scriptures of all religions and half an hour of meditation.

For further information write to Blue Mountain Center of Meditation, Box 381, Berkeley, Calif. 94701.

BUILDERS OF THE ADYTUM

Builders of the Adytum, functioning from its headquarters, the Temple of Tarot and Holy Qabalah, is the Aquarian Age repository and steward for the special system of mystical and occult teachings that is rooted in the Secret Wisdom of Israel, the Qabalah. Adytum stems from the Greek word meaning Holy of Holies, the Sanctum Sanctorum, The Holy Temple Within. Jesus was a carpenter, a builder—hence the name Builders of the Adytum (B.O.T.A.).

Members have lessons in Occult Psychology, Tarot, Holy Qabalah, Color and Sound, Spiritual Alchemy, and Esoteric Astrology mailed to them every other week.

For further information contact Builders of the Adytum, 5105 N. Figueroa St., Los Angeles, Calif. 90042; (213) 255-7141.

CALIFORNIA INSTITUTE OF ASIAN STUDIES
CULTURAL INTEGRATION FELLOWSHIP

The California Institute of Asian Studies is a graduate school specializing in Asian Culture and civilization and in East-West comparative studies in philosophy, religion, psychology, sociology, esthetics, and other humanistic disciplines. Since its inception in 1968 the Institute has made rapid progress by maintaining high academic standards and by advancing the cause of intercultural and international understanding.

Dr. Haridas Chaudhuri is president of the Institute. Classes are conducted in Meditation, Zen, the various Yogas, Sanskrit, Astrology, Buddhism, and other fields.

The Institute is a division of the Cultural Integration Fellowship, which was founded in San Francisco in 1951 as a nonprofit, nonsectarian organization devoted to universal religion, cultural understanding, and Creative self-unfoldment. The Ashram offers Sunday lectures by Dr. Chaudhuri, meditations, workshops, yoga demonstrations, and lectures on yoga and nutrition for balanced growth.

For further information contact the California Institute of Asian Studies, 3494 21st St., San Francisco, Calif. 94110; (415) 648–1489; or the Cultural Integration Fellowship, 2650 Fulton St., San Francisco, Calif. 94118; (415) 648–1489.

THE CENTER FOR THE STUDY OF DEMOCRATIC INSTITUTIONS

The Center for the Study of Democratic Institutions is a nonprofit educational institution dedicated to a continuing examination of the crucial issues facing humanity in an age of revolutionary change. In its efforts to foster the development of a civilization based on the power of reason, the center is committed to the spreading of exchanges of views by people with widely varying ideas.

Participants in center dialogues have included leaders in many fields in the United States—senators, governors, scientists, student leaders, lawyers, political scientists, skilled workmen from various trades, doctors, teachers—and leaders from a hundred other countries.

The center has sponsored three international convocations to examine the requirements for lasting peace—two of them based on the late Pope John's encyclical *Pace in Terris,* the third entitled *Pacem in Matibus* (peace in the oceans). Plans for future international meetings are being made.

For more information write to The Center for the Study of Democratic Institutions, P.O. Box 4068, Santa Barbara, Calif. 93103.

CHRISTANANDA ASHRAM

Christananda Ashram was established in 1966 by Yogiraj Evangelas Alexander as a satellite for anyone to visit or attend the classes in Hatha Yoga, Raja Yoga, lectures from the *Bhagavad-Gita, Upanishads, Yoga Sutra of Patanjali,* and the *Srimad-Gita.* Meditations are held daily and there is a family day every Sunday. Vegetarian food is served.

All religions are discussed and Yogiraj considers himself an inspirational tool for the student to become acquainted with different ideas. His work is to inspire the student to follow himself to the path of enlightenment.

For information write to: Christananda Ashram, 70 Hawthorn Way, San Jose, Calif. 95110.

CIMARRON ZEN CENTER

The Cimarron Zen Center is directed by Joshu Sasaki Roshi. It offers an intensive program consisting of chanting and za-zen. The day begins with group chanting and za-zen. On Tuesday, Wednesday, and Thursday, they also do afternoon za-zen.

For further information contact Cimarron Zen Center, 2505 Cimarron St., Los Angeles, Calif. 90018; (213) 732–2263.

Other Rinzai Centers directed by Sasaki Roshi are Mount Baldy Zen Center, P.O. Box 526, Mount Baldy, Calif. 91759; Redondo Beach Zen Center c/o Ron Olsen, 2305 Harriman La., Redondo Beach, Calif. 90278; Vancouver Zen Center of Rinzai-Ji, 139 Water St., Vancouver, B.C., Canada.

CLEAR THROUGH

Clear Through is an adult community that explores means of dissolving the veils of unconsciousness between individuals and that seeks means to direct experience of God-Consciousness. With equal souls, individual personalities and problems, they strive for Self-Realization and other realization. It was founded by William Welch.

For further information write to William Welch, 20362 Schoenbarn, Canoga Park, Calif. 91306.

COPTIC FELLOWSHIP OF AMERICA

The intent and purpose of the Coptic Fellowship of America is to teach basic philosophy of life; it has a religious foundation but is not sectarian. There is no obligation whatsoever except to study the lessons they send out every month to those who are interested in a Home Study Course. Regular meetings are held at the Los Angeles Temple and many other centers throughout the country.

For further information contact Coptic, 2015 Beverly Blvd., Los Angeles, Calif. 90057.

DIVINE LIGHT MISSION

Balyogeshwar Param Hans Satgurudev Shri Sant Ji Maharaj is at present only fourteen years old and it is claimed that he is a fully realized soul of our time. He began delivering discourses on the importance of the human body and meditation at the age of two and a half years to large assemblies.

Earning the grace of his own spiritual Master, the late Shri Hans Ji Maharaj, Balyogeshwar became a True Master or Satguru at the age of eight. Since that time, he has enlightened millions of souls to the Divine Light and Ineffable Name of God in India and thousands who have come to him from all over the world.

Balyogeshwar has proclaimed that the aim and purpose of his life is to spread the knowledge of the true nature of the soul to humanity as a whole. He declares that man has reached the apex of material prosperity while grossly neglecting spiritual evolution.

To advance and develop spiritually is the only way every human being can live cheerfully and spotlessly in this world of violence and oppression. To balance the material and scientific advancement of mankind, Balyogeshwar wants to further universal spiritual evolution.

For further information write to any of the following centers: Divine Light Mission, 3527 21st St., San Francisco, Calif. 94114; 6861 Alta Loma Terr., Los Angeles, Calif. 90028; 1560 Race St., Denver, Colo. 80206; 1429 Iris St., N.W., Washington, D.C. 20012.

EAST-WEST CULTURAL CENTER

The East-West Cultural Center is a nonprofit educational and religious organization. Its purpose is to teach and help integrate the cultural and spiritual values of East and West in order to create a greater world unity and a more progressive creative spiritual activity in the fields of education, the living arts, philosophy, and religion.

The inspiration for the center is the teachings of Sri Aurobindo. His vision of a divine life on earth and his saying, "The knowledge that unites is the true knowledge," are the guiding torchlights. The spiritual heart of the Center is the Jyoti Ashram, formed by leaders and lovers of Light who radiate Truth.

The center has a school conducted by Dr. Judith M. Tyberg, its founder and president, an Oriental library and a bookstore.

Also offered are yoga classes, music, poetry and study groups, and lectures by various religious teachers.

For additional information, write to East-West Cultural Center, 2865 W. Ninth St., Los Angeles, Calif. 90006.

ESALEN INSTITUTE

Esalen Institute is a center to explore those trends in the behavioral sciences, religion, and philosophy that emphasize the potentialities and values of human existence. Its activities consist of seminars and workshops, research and consulting programs, and a residential program that explores new directions in education and the behavioral sciences.

For information contact Esalen Institute, Big Sur, Calif. 93920; or Esalen Institute, 1776 Union St., San Francisco, Calif. 94123.

For a list of Growth Centers throughout the country write Association for Humanistic Psychology, 584 Page St., San Francisco, Calif. 94117.

HEALTHY HAPPY HOLY ORGANIZATION (3HO)

3HO was founded in 1968 by Yogi Bhajan, a Master of Kundalini Yoga, in the belief that the life-style for the Aquarian Age should be healthy, happy, and holy. Kundalini Yoga incorporates the disciplines of most other yogas but stresses awakening the kundalini, the primordial life energy under the navel point, and making it rise up the spine to the brain. This energizes and revitalizes all the seven "chakras" or psychic centers, and gives a permanent superior state of consciousness. Yogi Bhajan also emphasizes the importance of the breath and teaches "breath of fire," rapid rhythmic breathing with the aid of the diaphragm. 3HO is a rapidly expanding organization with ashrams throughout the United States and Canada. Extensive courses are offered during the year as well as several retreats.

For more information, contact 3HO National Headquarters, Guru Ram Dass Ashram, 8802 Melrose Ave., Los Angeles, Calif. 90069; (213) 274–6600; or 3HO North (Pacific Coast) Hargobind Sadan, Box 1051, San Rafael, Calif. 94902; (415) 453–0543.

HOLY ORDER OF MANS

The Holy Order of MANS is an organization of men and women who wish to promote a more thorough understanding of the divine laws of God and of Creation and the teachings of Lord Jesus Christ with the Ancient Christian Mysteries as a revealed teaching of this day, in accordance with the Testament and the quote of Lord Jesus that "all the mysteries shall be revealed."

The Order was conceived through revelation and evolved from the findings of a fact-finding group of professional people interested in the welfare of man for not only the present, but also for the future.

The word "MANS" is an acronym; its component words are of esoteric value. In San Francisco the Order is under the leadership of Dr. Earl W. Blighton. There are twelve Brotherhouses and twenty-six missionary stations in various cities across the United States.

For information write to Holy Order of MANS, 20 Steiner St., San Francisco, Calif. 94117.

THE HOPI WAY

The Hopi Way of Life is the Way of Peace. The New Age has made us aware of the spiritual way, the way within. It has also brought to the attention of mankind the ecological warning.

Andrew Hermequaftewa, Bluebird Chief of the Village of Shungopavi, says, "Boastful people cannot become part of Hopi Village. Only those who desire to live peacefully, to harm no one, are admitted into the religious order of the village life. People should not disregard each other. There should be respect between all peoples."

For his statement to Congress and other information on the Hopi Prophecies, write to Hopi Friendship Association, 119 Quapaw St., Santa Fe, N.M. 87501.

THE HOUSE OF LOVE AND PRAYER

Yeshivah means sitting. Yeshivah is a place you come on your journey and stay for a while. Yeshivah is a place to sit and study the Torah (the Teaching, the Way).

The House of Love and Prayer is where you learn to open the doors to your heart and your mind and your soul. This yeshivah is different from any you've seen or heard about and you will fail the course if you learn only what is in the book. According to the tradition, any word which is truly holy speaks on three levels: the fact, the story, and the melody. The fact reaches only as far as the mind. The story reaches as far as the heart. And the melody reaches all the way to the soul. In this yeshivah you pass only when you learn the melody. When you know it deeply you sing it wherever you are, whatever you are doing.

In 1968 Rabbi Schlomo Carlebach, together with some of his followers, started the House of Love and Prayer in San Francisco. It was his dream that there should be a house of Abraham in the world, where the doors never closed and all the hungry people of the world were invited: people who were hungry for bread; people who were hungry for love; people who were hungry for light. He said, "My definition of a House of Love and Prayer is, when you walk in, someone loves you; when you walk out, someone misses you."

The House of Love and Prayer has been a place for people to come and go. During the few years of its existence, the House has gathered together a group of young people ready for the next step: to build a place where people can come and stay for a while. They are calling this place the Town of Love and Prayer.

For additional information, contact the House of Love and Prayer, 1456 Ninth Ave., San Francisco, Calif. 94122; (415) 921–2575.

INNER RESEARCH INSTITUTE

Tai Chi classes at the Inner Research Institute are given under the direction of headmaster Ch'u-Fang Chu.

For further information, contact the Inner Research Institute, 131 Hayes St., San Francisco, Calif. 94128; (415) 621–2681.

INSTITUTE OF ABILITY

Charles and Ava Berner founded the Institute of Ability to help individuals increase their ability to live life better in their own estimation. The Institute is also the organizational vehicle for Abilitism, a new "religion" that holds that each of us has divine ability and that our purpose in life is the fulfillment of our relationships with each other through experiencing understanding and being totally conscious of each other.

A new discovery of Abilitism has resulted in making self-enlightenment and the Life enlightenment that fol-after truth in from three to ten days. Amazingly, this self-enlightenment and the Life enlightenment that follows are the same type that Buddha attained. New deep relating techniques and knowledge have made this possible and have also resulted in a whole new relating yoga. Correspondence courses are taught; Enlightenment and Relating Intensives given, and ministers trained at their seminary and at many branches throughout the United States.

For additional information contact the Institute of Ability, World Headquarters, Box 798, End of Crystal Creek Road, Lucerne Valley, Calif. 92356; (714) 248–7007.

INTEGRAL YOGA INSTITUTE

"A body of perfect health and strength, mind with all clarity and calmness, intellect as sharp as a razor, will as pliable as steel, heart full of love and compassion, Life full of dedication and Realization of the True Self is the goal of Integral Yoga. Attain this through asanas, pranayama, chanting of Holy Names, self-discipline, selfless action, mantra, japa, meditation, study and reflection.

Om, shanti, shanti, shanti

Ever yours in Yoga."

Swami Satchidananda

Every three months, Swami Satchidananda visits the West Coast ashrams. There is meditation each morning and a chanting and meditation on Wednesday evening. Sunday is family day.

For information about Hatha Yoga classes, vegetarian cooking, Raja Yoga and Gita classes contact the Integral Yoga Institute, 770 Dolores St., San Francisco, Calif. 94110; (415) 826–8119. Integral Yoga is also at 1905 Grove St., Berkeley 94704; (415) 841–1160; and at 311 Ocean View Ave., Santa Cruz 95060.

INTERNATIONAL COOPERATION COUNCIL—THE COOPERATORS

The International Cooperation Council (ICC) is a non-profit coordinating body of autonomous individuals and groups, each seeking in its own way to contribute constructively to the global transformation of our time. Based upon the principle of "unity in diversity among all peoples," ICC is an experiment whose goal is to foster the emergence of a new universal man and civilization serving the well-being of all mankind.

Utilizing the methods and knowledge of modern science in concert with valid insights of religion, philosophy, and the arts, the creative activities of ICC cover a spectrum from the search into man's inner nature to dynamic social action. Eighty groups are now cooperating with ICC.

The Cooperators believe that if man had a broader view of the meaning of his existence, he would begin to realize the pettiness and the triviality of the deadly competition that is responsible for most of his present troubles—war, race conflicts, pollution of nature, famine, and starvation. What is required is a change in human nature. Cooperation must eventually replace competition.

Interim projects of The Cooperators include: 1) cooperation between science and religion in the study of the evolution of man's psychic structure and its survival of bodily death, 2) the establishment of a "World Authority" capable of enforcing peaceful relations between all nations, 3) eliminating the original source of competition by providing sufficient food to supply all mankind, and 4) arousing the women of the world to use their power to obtain peace.

For more information contact 17819 Roscoe Blvd., Northridge, Calif. 91324.

INSTITUTE FOR THE DEVELOPMENT OF THE HARMONIOUS HUMAN BEING, INC.

The attainment of a conscious state is not an accidental occurrence. It makes no difference what system of development a serious seeker chooses. What is important is how a person applies himself toward the aim to be achieved. Every system of development, no matter what its professed aim, states, "know thyself." A school is a living being which exists according to the time, place, and people. Once a school has served its purpose, it is dismantled; nothing lasts forever.

The Institute for the Development of the Harmonious Human Being is a fourth-way school which uses the ideas and techniques of many different systems of development. Our aim is to inform prospective students of the possibilities open to their limited psyches and to supply conditions for self-study once these possibilities are realized.

For further information contact the Institute for the Development of the Harmonious Human Being, 6311 Yucca St., Los Angeles, Calif. 90028.

INTERNATIONAL I CHING STUDIES INSTITUTE—TAOIST SANCTUARY

I Ching Studies aim at developing a fuller awareness of the life miracle you are experiencing. With heightened consciousness, one is able to live more effectively. *I Ching,* through the use of archetypes, defines the continual ongoing changes that make up life in a way that helps you to discern your truth, whatever it may be, so that you can express it more completely and more joyously.

Lectures on the *Book of Changes* and *I Ching* workshops are offered. Tai Chi instruction is also available.

Tai Chi Ch'uan is a ritual of health developed in ancient China, based upon the ageless symbol of man's inner self— the Tai Chi Tu. These exercises can be practiced by the young and old, weak and strong since they do not depend upon muscular power but upon soft circular movements, movements so beautiful and rhythmical that they are a pleasure to practice.

This ancient discipline generates physical, mental, and spiritual energy and is taught in the authoritative tradition.

The International I Ching Studies Institute is a related activity of the Taoist Sanctuary.

For additional information, write to the International I Ching Studies Institute, 10985 Bluffside Dr., Studio City, Calif. 91604.

INTERNATIONAL NEW THOUGHT ALLIANCE

New Thought is a synonym for growth, development, and perpetual progress. It recognizes a superiority and excellence in man; it does not deal with limitations; it sets no bounds to the soul's progress; for it sees in each soul transcendental faculties as limitless as infinity itself.

New Thought may be said to possess a fixed ideal, that of an eternal search for Truth. The adherents of New Thought worship the omnipresent God, the indwelling God, in whom we live, move and have our being. They do not conceive of God as distant or separated from man, but as a universal spirit permeating all nature, finding its highest expression in man.

The International New Thought Alliance is a year-round working organization, democratic in structure, that serves as the medium through which all metaphysical schools, churches, and centers can work together. Its message is destined to lead the world into a higher consciousness, even the God-consciousness in man.

For further information, write to the International New Thought Alliance, 7033 Sunset Blvd., Hollywood, Calif. 90028.

INTERNATIONAL SIVANANDA YOGA SOCIETY

The Society is a nonprofit organization whose sole purpose is to propagate the teaching of Yoga to those seeking its benefits. Their goal is to help each individual find health, happiness and inner peace through Yoga. Their headquarters is an ashram in Val Morin, Canada, in the Laurentian Mountains. They also have a Yoga retreat in Nassau on Paradise Island and a Yoga farm in Grass Valley, California, in the foothills of the Sierras. Classes are conducted personally by Swami Vishnu-Devananda.

Swami Sivananda is the spiritual power behind the organization. His eagerness to serve all led him from a successful career as a dedicated and renowned medical doctor to offer himself as a servant of God. During his life, he was hailed throughout the world as one of the greatest Saints and Yogis of modern time.

Swami Vishnu-Devananda was one of Sivananda's closest disciples. After many years of study and service in the Himalayas, Swami was sent on a world tour as Sivananda's "messenger to the West."

For additional information, contact International Sivananda Yoga Society, 1738½ Ninth Ave., San Francisco, Calif. 94122; (415) 564–2497; or Vrindavan, 803 Route 1, Grass Valley, Calif. 95945; (415) 273–7667.

KAILAS SHUGENDO

Dr. Neville Warwick teaches the yoga of fire walking, which is said to be an integration with one's soul. A twenty-foot-square area is roped off and pieces of white paper are torn and attached to the ropes on four sides, which designates this as a holy place. A fire pit dug and a bridge of thin logs is arranged over the pit. Kindling is placed in the pit and the fire started. On each piece of kindling is written, "I pray safe and beneficent hot coals walking."

The symbol worn on their clothes and the bandanas is the three-legged crow of Mount Haguro surrounded by flames. A mala, which is a string of 108 beads and a guru (or Meru) bead, is worn around their necks and used for the saying of mantra. The guru bead is usually the same as all the other beads except that it is centrally located. Dr. Warwick and his followers have a skull as their guru bead and say it is there to remind them to attain enlightenment in this life.

Hiwatari, or fire treading, is practiced once a week by Dr. Warwick and his students on an open beach or in the mountains. Dr. Warwick makes a thousand passes over the fire holding a mala and saying a mantra. He also instructs his students how to control the fire and eliminate excess smoke.

Other practices are jumping into ice cold waterfalls and

SWAMI SIVANANDA

❝Worship the Lord with intense
faith and aspiration and
He will surely bestow His
grace upon you.❞

mountain climbing. Puja ceremony is performed twice a day.

For more information, write to Dr. Neville Warwick, 2362 Pine St., San Francisco, Calif. 94115; (415) 921–2771.

KRISHNAMURTI FOUNDATION OF AMERICA

The Krishnamurti Foundation, a charitable trust with tax exempt status, was founded for the purpose of making the teachings of J. Krishnamurti available to the public through publications, films and recordings and to sponsor his public talks in the United States and elsewhere.

Among the many issues with which Krishnamurti is concerned, the need for change is central. "We need a totally different kind of society," he says. "One of the greatest problems we have is the urgency for a fundamental revolution in ourselves, a radical change in the way of our thinking, feeling and reacting." Pointing to the chaos and destruction that threatens our world, Krishnamurti insists on the need for every serious person to understand himself without illusion. Only in this way can there be the awakening of a new mind and a different way of living.

For information about Krishnamurti and his work, write to: Krishnamurti Foundation of America, P.O. Box 216, Ojai, California 93023.

In 1968, a Krishnamurti Foundation was established in London, England. It issues a bulletin with information about Krishnamurti's worldwide activities, and maintains the school and adult center at Brockwood Park, Bramdean, Hampshire, where Krishnamurti spends many months each year with the students and staff.

For information, write to Krishnamurti Foundation, 24 Southend Rd., Beckenham, Kent, BR 3 ISD; Secretary: Ms. Mary Cadogan.

MAGANA AND WALT BAPTISTE SAN FRANCISCO YOGA INSTITUTE

The Magana and Walt Baptiste Yoga Institute offers the practices that lead to self-realization and then to God-realization. Detailed instruction in controlled fasting, health, and diet is given; there is instruction in graded weight-lifting for physical strength and endurance; Hatha, Prana, Kriya, Karma and Raja Yoga for suppleness, vitality, and awakening of the subtle senses; meditation, modern, primitive, Eastern, and Near Eastern dance courses by Magana for grace and development of body rhythms.

For more information, contact Magana and Walt Baptiste San Francisco Yoga Institute, 149 Powell St., San Francisco, Calif. 94102; (415) 362–2338.

MAITREYAN MAN LIVE-IN CENTER

Karl Heussenstamm has begun meetings that focus on the meaning of Maitreyan (universal) man and the possibility of a live-in center to develop this as a life-style. Those who wish to inquire about this effort are invited to write him at 11963 Walnut La., Los Angeles, Calif. 90025.

MAZDAZNAN

The Mazdaznan Teaching is based on the original teachings of Zarathustra (also known as Zoroaster) who lived six thousand years before Christ. He was the first of a long line of Zarathustras; the last one lived six hundred years before Christ. Mazdaznans are concerned only with the pure teaching of the first Zarathustra.

Dr. Otoman Zar-Adusht Ha'nish was sent by the Inner Temple Community of El Khaman to bring this message to the world. This inner community is located in the Himalayan range of mountains. In this community Dr. O. Z. A. Hanish had access to the original writings of the first Zarathustra, the pure teaching without all the embellishments that have been added through the centuries by other Zarathustras.

The name of Mazdaznan is the original Zend name used by Zarathustra. It means "the thought that masters all things" or "the God thought that underlies all things."

Dr Hanish came to the Western world in approximately

1850 and taught until February 29, 1936, when he passed on, to return to higher realms. There is one thought he always stressed: "The important thing is the teaching and not the messenger."

The purpose of the Mazdaznan Teaching could be stated in these few words: The spirit of God dwells within the innermost heart of each human being, and this God spirit is perfect. We are to be in the body what we are already in the spirit. We accomplish this through the use of rhythmic breathing exercises, diet, song, and prayers, to refine our body which is the instrument through which the God spirit can reveal itself in ever increasing measure in proportion to the effort the individual makes toward this goal.

Among our invocations is one that expresses the purpose of our existence here on Earth, expressed by Ainyahita nine thousand years ago: "That we are here upon this earth, to reclaim the earth, to turn the desert into a paradise, a paradise most suitable unto God and his associates to dwell therein."

It was not until 1902 that Dr. Hanish organized the teaching in New York City under the name of Mazdaznan. Later the headquarters was moved to Chicago where it was known under the name of "The Reorganized Mazdaznan Temple Association." In 1916 it moved to Los Angeles, California, where it is still located.

Mazdaznan is a worldwide organization represented in twenty-two countries with its International Headquarters at 1159 S. Norton Ave., Los Angeles, Calif. 90019.

MEDITATION

A weekly meditation evening is held at the home of Bob Raymer, a disciple of Yogananda Paramahansa who has since been close to Satya Sai Baba and Swami Muktananda. The evening concentrates on meditation with some chanting and talk. It is open to any follower of any guru and all true seekers.

For information write to Bob Raymer, 795 S. Napoli Dr., Pacific Palisades, Calif. 90272.

MEETING OF THE WAYS

Meeting of the Ways first came together in June 1971 at Live Oak Park in Berkeley as a festive gathering of local spiritual groups. Their purpose is to discover through dialogue the unity underlying the different approaches to spiritual living. As no one has a monopoly on being in the here and now, they are seeking to show how each tradition and each Master plays one of the many melodies of Universal Truth.

In order to achieve fuller communication within and without the emerging spiritual community, Meeting of the Ways inaugurated a radio program of the same name in August 1971. Every week, on Saturdays from 8 to 10 P.M. on KQED–FM, a participating member organization has the opportunity to present a high-quality broadcast to the expanding listening public.

Programs have been presented by the Ananda Marga, followers of Dadaji, the House of Love and Prayer of Rabbi Schlomo Carlebach, the disciples of Swami Satchidananda at the Integral Yoga Institute, Ajare Neville Warwick and the Kailas Shugendo Yamabushi, Yogi Bhajan's Healthy Happy Holy Organization, the students of Sant Keshavadas and Swami Chinmayananda at the Lokoya Thapovan, the Ruhani Satsang followers of Sant Kirpal Singh, Maharishi Mahesh Yogi's Students International Meditation Society, Sri Chinmoy and his students, the followers of Sufi Sam Lewis and Pir Vilayat Inayat Khan, the Universal Great Brotherhood founded by Dr. Serge Raynaud de la Ferriere, the Wailua University of Contemplative Arts of Master Subramuniya, and the Walt Baptiste San Francisco Yoga Institute. Other groups and Masters will be on the program in the future.

Taping of special events has been done but, for the most part, all programs are live.

If you would like information as to how to be on the program or how to start a similar project in your area, write to Sudharshan, 35 Dorland St., San Francisco, Calif. 94110.

MEHER BABA

Meher Baba means "Compassionate Father" and is the name given by a group of early disciples to their Master when they were first drawn to him. Born in India in 1894, Baba began to attract considerable attention and a growing number of followers when, in the early 1920s, signs of his spiritual status first became apparent.

Meher Baba stated explicitly that he is "the Ancient One," that is, the God-Man whose advent is anticipated in many of today's religious and mystical traditions. Most commonly in India he is referred to as the "Avatar," a Hindu word meaning "descendant of God." The view of mysticism, however, whether Eastern or Western, is that the appearance of the Avatar is not a one-time event in history, but rather a periodic occurrence on earth.

"All religions are equal to me. And all castes and creeds are dear to me. But though I appreciate all 'isms,' religions and political parties for the many good things they seek to achieve, I do not and cannot belong to any of these 'isms,' religions or political parties, for the absolute Truth, while equally including them, transcends all of them and leaves no room for separative divisions which are all equally false."

Baba gives no rituals or ceremonies, no particular diets or exercises, no specific form of meditation to his followers. There are no "churches," no designated teachers. There is no fee. True religion, in Baba's eyes, is not a card-carrying affair but rather a matter of "the heart," the degree to which one lives an honest and loving life.

During his colorful and enigmatic life, which included forty-four years of verbal silence from 1925 until he passed away, Meher Baba awakened innumerable people around the world to quest for higher consciousness and their own Infinite Reality. Although he frequently stated, "I have not come to teach but to awaken," Baba has given a great number of original explanations and discourses concerning the dynamics of spiritual advancement which are published in a variety of books.

A list of books by and about Meher Baba, together with

❝The only real Existence
is that of the One and only
God, who is the Self
in every self.**❞**

MEHER BABA

more information about him, can be obtained by writing to Meher Baba Information, Box 1101, Berkeley, Calif. 94701. Details of various informal meetings and other activities around the country can also be obtained from this information center.

NICHIREN SHOSHU OF AMERICA

Nichiren Shoshu of America is a philosophy of happiness. It is a growing organization of individuals united by one common goal, World Peace. The ideal of peace begins within each person's own life first, improving his job, his health, his family relationships, and his own character. It is a true revolution based on the human being instead of only changes in society.

The philosophy itself is a practical one, based on the teachings of Nichiren Daishonin who first propagated True Buddhism in Japan seven hundred years ago. The basic practice is done individually in the home and involves chanting *Nam-myoho-renge-kyo* to the Gohonzon, a scroll on which a perfect condition of life for the human being is inscribed. This daily practice generates great vital life-force, wisdom, and good fortune for the individual, and enables him to grow to victory in daily affairs.

Nichiren Shoshu has grown to a membership of nearly 200,000 in the United States. Many people who join are unfamiliar with this philosophy. The image of the Buddhist, robed, shaven head; the temples and the mysticism are not present at the discussion meeting. Instead, they see well-groomed people of all ages ranging from a student to a bus driver to a doctor.

Nichiren Shoshu is evident in almost every country in the world. Culturally, the organization sponsors numerous parades, shows and an annual All-American Convention held in different cities. Through the organization, people are creating happy daily lives and families, and are seeing real progress toward their goal of World Peace. Activity Centers are located in Santa Monica, West Los Angeles, San Diego, San Francisco, Honolulu, Seattle, Denver, Dallas, Chicago, New York, Boston, Washington, D.C., and Mexico City. Temples are maintained for religious ceremonies in Etiwanda, California, and Honolulu.

Group pilgrimages are made to the Nichiren Shoshu Head Temple, Daisekiji, a the foot of Mount Fuji in Japan.

The *World Tribune,* published three times weekly, is the principal English language publication. The *Seikyo Times* is a monthly study magazine.

For additional information write to Nichiren Shoshu of America, America Headquarters, 1351 Ocean Front, Santa Monica, Calif. 90401; (213) 870–7373.

THE PHILOSOPHICAL RESEARCH SOCIETY, INC.

Founded by Manly P. Hall in 1934, the purpose of the Society is to make discoveries about the nature of man by researching in the special areas of philosophy, comparative religion, and psychology. The Society holds regular meetings and has numerous publications. It also has a research library of 5,000 volumes and an unusual collection of art symbolizing the nature of man.

For further information contact The Philosophical Research Society, Inc., 3910 Los Feliz Blvd, Los Angeles, Calif. 90027.

PSYCHOSYNTHESIS INSTITUTE

Psychosynthesis is an inclusive and positive conception of man that considers him dynamically as a being in a process of personal growth within an evolving universe. It is a comprehensive psychological method that includes the self as well as the libido, the imagination as well as the complexes, the will as well as the instinctual drives. More than a theory, it is a way of looking at the mystery of man, his inner life, his psyche; it is a practical method that can include many of the specific approaches to personal growth currently entering the mainstream of psychology and education. These methods are unified around the notion of a self at the core of each individual that can direct the harmonious development and integration of all aspects of the personality. Beyond that personal harmony lies access to higher realms: creativity, transpersonal experience and spiritual development.

The Psychosynthesis Institute offers a wide program of individual sessions, group workshops, and lectures as well as training for professionals in the theory and practice of psychosynthesis. Publications on psychosynthesis and related areas are issued periodically. A current publication list and calendar of activities are available.

For further information contact the Psychosynthesis Institute, 150 Doherty Way, Redwood City, Calif. 94062; (415) 365–7941.

RADHA SOAMI

In recent years many Saints known to history, such as Kabir Sahib, Tulsi Das, Shamas Tabriz, Maulana Rum, and Guru Nanak together with his nine successors, have been the chief exponents of the teachings of the Saints.

The present Master of this line is Sardar Charan Singh Grewal. Disciples may come to his haven on earth at no charge in order to renew and refresh themselves. Darshan is given daily. A sincere desire to understand the true meaning and purpose of human life is all that is required of a seeker to become a Satsangi.

There are home and community Satsangs throughout the country where devotees chant, meditate, and work together. A monthly newsletter is available on request. A listing of the various locations of Satsangs is also available.

For further information on Satsangs or the writings of Charan Singh, write to Radha Soami Foundation, Beas, P.O. Box 7667, Riverside, Calif. 92503.

THE ROSICRUCIANS

Is there a concealed wisdom that can lead to the mystery of life, one that the troubled Western world sorely needs? As a civilization, we have come a long way. But we stand upon the achievements of the ancients. In the past there were men whose vision was vaster than that of others and who had a power of accomplishment far greater. Such men were ahead of their times. Bigotry and intolerance forced these sages to band together, to secrete and preserve their accumulated wisdom.

Out of the ancient lands of the East have leaked strange tales. They tell of the miraculous powers and knowledge of these brotherhoods of sages. Are these tales fact or fancy?

The Rosicrucians, as a centuries-old fraternity, have conducted an extensive search into these remote lands. They have returned with enlightening and startling truths long secretly cherished.

Regardless of race, religion, social conditions, or locality, you can share the privileges of membership.

For information contact The Rosicrucians, AMORC, Rosicrucian Park, San Jose, Calif. 95114.

RUHANI SATSANG (Path of the Masters)

Ruhani Satsang is an inner science of the soul and consists of contracting the soul with the Oversoul with the help and guidance of a living spiritual adept.

At the time of initiation, the present living Master, Satguru Kirpal Singh Ji, gives to the initiate an actual experience of rising above body consciousness. This initial experience, however rudimentary, of attunement to the inner spiritual lights and sounds that drag the soul into the Beyond may be developed daily by a program of meditation as enjoined by the Master. The spiritual aspirant is further counseled to weed out all undesirable and self-limiting traits in his make-up, traits that obstruct his spiritual development. A daily diary of lapses is maintained by the aspirant to make him fully conscious of his weaknesses. Once an aspirant has been initiated by a true Master, he is given constant guidance and protection both in his inner and outer development.

Open meetings of Ruhani Satsang are held on Sundays in the areas listed below. The hour-long meetings consist of readings from Sant Kirpal Singh's writings and, occasionally, tapes and movies of the Master. The meetings are open to all except small children. Books and literature by the Master are available.

The San Francisco meetings are held the second, fourth, and, when possible, fifth Sundays of each month at 756 Union Street (intersection).

For additional information, contact Stuart and Sheila Judd, 984 Oxford St., Berkeley, Calif. 94707; (415) 526–8050.

For a directory of Satsangs throughout the country, write to National Headquarters, P.O. Box 3037, Anaheim, Calif. 92803.

S.A.B.A.

The Sino-American Buddhist Association, under the direction of the Abbot-To Lun, combines sutra study, meditation, and recitation to increase the understanding of the principles and practice of the Dharma. Lectures every evening cover important Buddhist texts. Mantras are also chanted.

For further information, contact S.A.B.A., 1731 15th St., San Francisco, Calif. 94103; (415) 621–5202.

SAI BABA CENTER—INDRA DEVI YOGA FOUNDATION

The Sai Baba Center in Los Angeles was formed by Richard and Janet Bock for the purpose of devotion toward Guru and God. On Thursday evenings a Hatha Yoga class, conducted by Robert Silver, a disciple of Indra Devi, is offered. Then bajans (devotional songs to Guru and God) are sung. The chanting is followed by a meditation and discourse.

Friday evenings begin with the chanting of bajans and a tape of Sai Baba or a guest lecturer is then heard. Often films on Sai Baba are shown.

The Center has a bookstore with photographs, books, and records of Sai Baba.

Indra Devi is a great devotee of Sai Baba. She has beautiful land near the Mexican border where she holds classes for teacher-training in Hatha Yoga. On the grounds is a temple for Sai Baba and an organic garden.

For further information on Sai Baba or the Indra Devi

❝REALIZE
and then help others to
REALIZE.❞

SATHYA SAI BABA

Foundation, contact Sai Baba Center, 7720 Sunset Blvd., Los Angeles, Calif. 90046; (213) 876–5019.

SELF-REALIZATION FELLOWSHIP

"Self-realization is the knowing—in body, mind, and soul—that we are one with the omnipresence of God; that we do not have to pray that it comes to us, that we are not merely near it at all times, but that God's omnipresence is our omnipresence; that we are just as much a part of Him now as we ever will be. All we have to do is to improve our knowing" (Paramahansa Yogananda).

The aim of Self-Realization is to disseminate among the nations a knowledge of definite scientific techniques for attaining direct personal experience of God.

The techniques of the science of Yoga have been used for millennia, with exact and known results, by Saints and great Masters of India. Paramahansa Yogananda, a great Master of modern India, established Self-Realization Fellowship to spread the practice of the ancient yoga science in the West.

Self-Realization Fellowship shows a balanced way to attune body, mind, and soul to cosmic laws of life, and thus overcome the threefold suffering of man: physical disease, mental inharmonies, and spiritual ignorance.

Jesus said, "Thou shalt love the Lord thy God with all thy heart, and with all thy soul, and with all thy mind, and with all thy strength" (Mark 12:30). Self-Realization Fellowship teaches the scientific yoga methods by which man may bring all his powers to the altar of God, in accordance with Christ's command.

The techniques enable the sincere devotee to attune himself to the ever-present help of Jesus Christ and of the great Masters of wisdom who established Self-Realization Fellowship.

The Self-Realization technique of Kriya Yoga, the world's most ancient universal science for God-communion, was taught in India by the prophet Krishna 3,100 years before the Christian era. In the *Bhagavad-Gita*, India's Bible, Lord Krishna said, "The yogi is greater than body-

PARAMAHANSA YOGANANDA

66Seek spiritual riches first.
When you have gained
inner joy, you will see
that material well-being
follows naturally.99

disciplining ascetics, greater even than the followers of the path of wisdom (Jnana Yoga) or of the path of action (Karma Yoga); be thou, O disciple, a yogi!" (VI:46).

That Christ taught Yoga methods to his close disciples to aid in their redemption is revealed in the little understood book of Revelation in the Bible. There, St. John speaks of seven stars and seven churches. These symbols refer to the seven *chakras* or centers of light in man's cerebrospinal axis, explained in Yoga treatises as the seven divinely planned exits or "trap doors" through which a devotee, by meditation, may escape by seven successive steps into Cosmic Consciousness. Thus, he frees himself scientifically from the otherwise inescapable conviction that he is merely a body-bound mortal, subject to inexorable laws of the material universe.

The teachings given by Paramahansa Yogananda to the modern world reveal the underlying harmony of the original Christianity as taught by Christ and the original Yoga as taught by Krishna.

A Self-Realization Fellowship publishing center is located in Los Angeles.

Self-Realization Fellowship temples in California are located in Hollywood, Pacific Palisades, Fullerton, Encinitas, and San Diego. Services are held on Sundays.

For information about services write to Mother Center and International Headquarters of Self-Realization Fellowship, 3880 San Rafael Ave., Los Angeles, Calif. 90065; (213) 225-2471.

SELF-REALIZATION LAKE SHRINE

The Lake Shrine was opened in 1950 by Paramahansa Yogananda to refresh the mind and spirit in an atmosphere of peace and harmony. The site has a two-acre natural lake, encircled by verdant hills and is within the city limits of Los Angeles. The shores are planted with tropical fruit trees and luxuriant vegetation. An open-air temple with unique golden-lotus columns faces the calm waters of the lake. Nearby is the Gandhi World Peace Memorial, an ancient Chinese sarcophagus containing a portion of the

Mahatma's ashes. Divine services are held every Sunday in the chapel. A Mississippi houseboat is used as a Sunday school. An island of tropical plantings where swans and other water birds nest adds to the beauty of the area. The grass area near Gandhi's ashes is a perfect place to sit, meditate or chant. On the grounds is a bookstore, Yogananda Museum and an Indian Gift Shop.

For further information contact the Self-Realization Lake Shrine, 17190 Sunset Blvd., Pacific Palisades, Calif. 90272; (213) 454–4114.

SHEPHERD'S BUSH

Shepherd's Bush is a Metaphysical Center for study and counseling and offers seminars on Tarot, astrology, mysticism and music, Sufi meditation, and Yoga.

Shepherd's Bush means a place of the way, the way being up into the higher consciousness where the creative source dwells.

For further information, contact Shepherd's Bush, 5416 Gaston Ave., Dallas, Tex. 75214.

THE SOCIETY FOR COMPARATIVE PHILOSOPHY, INC.

The Society for Comparative Philosophy is an educational, nonprofit corporation formed with the initial purpose of assisting the research, writing, and lectures of Alan Watts on the fruitful interchange of ideas and experiences between the philosophies of Asia and the West, and to aid and sponsor other individuals and groups in related activities.

"Philosophy" is used in the title of this Society in its older and most inclusive sense; it means not only the study of logic, and speculations about matters of being, knowing, aesthetics, and ethics, but also "natural philosophy" as this phrase was once used to include the various sciences now called physics, chemistry, astronomy, biology, psychology, and the rest. For it is becoming more and more obvious that our knowledge of the world cannot be set rigidly in departments, and that we are in great need of exchanges, not only between disciplines and fields of knowledge, but also between the ideas of differing cultures.

Therefore the special interests of the Society are: 1) Comparative studies of the philosophies, religions, and social institutions of East and West, and also of so-called primitive and civilized societies. 2) Studies of man's relation to nature and the universe, including problems of ecology and conservation, so as to promote awareness of man's inseparable union with the universe as a whole and of the necessity of respecting it as an integral and major part of his own existence. 3) Research and experiment on the nature and the various forms of human consciousness. We are interested in ways of *feeling* that the individual is not a "stranger on the earth" but a particular action of the entire universe at the point which each person calls "here," "now," and "I." 4) Ways and means of enabling technology to be a cooperation, instead of a conflict, with our natural environment, having the fullest respect for the conservation of resources and the balance of nature. 5) Man's religious, psychological, and moral adaptation to a world in which social changes are coming about with ever-increasing rapidity, requiring that he learn to "swim" in a universe of flux and relativity, instead of trying to "stand" on the crumbling rocks of intellectual and moral absolutes.

A complete list of Alan Watts's tape recordings is available from MEA, Box 303, Sausalito, Calif. 94965.

For further information contact S.C.P., Inc. P.O. Box 857, Sausalito, Calif. 94965.

SHREE GURUDEV SIDDHA YOGA ASHRAM

The S.G.S.Y. Ashram was started under the auspices of Swami Muktananda by Donald and Diane Harrison in March 1971. It was established to worship Baba Muktananda as the Divine Consciousness. Swami Muktananda is the spiritual head of the Shree Gurudev Ashram of Ganeshpuri, India. He is an adept master of Siddha Yoga and has attracted a growing following of seekers of inner peace and enlightenment from all over India and abroad.

His mission is to awaken divine consciousness in an aspirant by means of Shaktipat initiation and thereby further his spiritual development.

The San Francisco Ashram is located in Piedmont in the hills above Oakland. Daily meditations are held. The evening's activities include group meditation, kirtan, tapes, and occasionally films of the ashram in India.

OM NAMAH SHIVAYA

For further information contact Shree Gurudev Siddha Yoga Ashram, 27 Highland Ave., Piedmont, Calif. 94611; (415) 655–5838 or 563–4195.

SIVANANDA YOGA CENTER

Swami Sivananda is the spiritual power behind the organization under the supervision of Swami Vishnu-Devananda.

Yoga is a way of complete life. There are a number of different subdivisions in Yoga, but only one Yoga, with all paths leading to the same goal. Some teachers advise students to follow one path ignoring the others. We feel that following a synthesis of all Yoga techniques is best suited for rapid progress. There are five requisites for this Yogic life: 1) proper exercise, 2) proper breathing, 3) proper diet, 4) relaxation, and 5) positive thinking and meditation. Regular day and evening classes are given here, and lectures in the philosophy are held on Sunday evenings.

There are Sivananda Yoga Centers throughout the United States. For information about the center nearest you or the Yoga Camps in Val Morin, Canada, or on Paradise Island, Nassau, Bahamas, write to Sivananda Yoga Center, 115 N. Larchmont Blvd., Los Angeles, Calif. 90004; (213) 464–1276.

S.I.M.S.—MAHARISHI YOGI

Transcendental meditation is a safe, scientific, and natural technique that develops the full potential of the mind. It allows the mind to systematically transcend the subtle states of the thought process and consciously arrive at the source of thought, an inexhaustible reservoir of energy and creative intelligence. The technique is taught individually so that each student may develop the full potential of his mind. Transcendental meditation involves no concentration or contemplation. It simply uses the natural tendency of the mind to seek a field of greater happiness and fulfillment.

For information about the center nearest you write to Students' International Meditation Society, 2728 Channing Way, Berkeley, Calif. 94704 (National Headquarters); or 1015 Gayley Avenue, Los Angeles, Calif. 90024.

S.R.M.

S.R.M. is transcendental meditation as taught by Maharishi Mahesh Yogi. Introductory classes are given by Charles F. Lutes, president of S.R.M., every Tuesday evening at the S.R.M. Auditorium, 11428 Santa Monica Blvd., W. Los Angeles.

For additional information phone (213) 479–6911 or 879–0289.

STILLPOINT FOUNDATION

The Stillpoint Foundation is run by Gia Fu Feng and offers daily meditations. Classes are also given in pottery, crafts, shiatsu, massage, calligraphy, painting, and oracle reading from the original Chinese I Ching. For more information write to the Stillpoint Foundation, 20300 Bear Creak Rd., Los Gatos, Calif. 95030.

SUFI ORDER

The Sufi Order is an ancient esoteric school of initiates embracing all religions in which training in meditation is given to seek and find God the Creator in creation. Sufism is the way of love, harmony, and beauty.

Pir Vilayat Khan is the head of the Sufi Order in the West, which was founded by his father Pir-O-Murshid

❝I am a tide in the sea
of life, bearing towards
the shore all who come
within my enfoldment.❞

Hazrat Inayat Khan. Pir Vilayat is also president of the International School for Esoteric Studies.

One meditation monthly is held on the first Tuesday of every month at the East-West Cultural Center, 2865 West Ninth Street in Los Angeles. Often a tape of one of Pir Vilayat's lectures is played. When in town Pir Vilayat lectures and holds seminars and retreats where the emphasis is on meditation.

For more information contact Ms. Suzanne d'Mitrieff, 6904 Radford Ave., N. Hollywood, Calif. 91605; (213) 765–2895.

SUFI PATH

The life of the Bay Area Center is taken up primarily with the practice of definite and regular meetings; it is important that they be conducted in an over-all rhythmic pattern or sequence. There are meetings for disciples only; the Sufi Path is Initiatic, both formally and esoterically, and this makes it possible that discipleship be a serious, though not necessarily burdensome, endeavor. The study of the Gathas (esoteric study lessons) is basic to the broader implementation of the Grand View and Being of Sufism as Hazrat Pir-O-Murshid Inayat Khan has taught.

The public meetings are a special consideration. On Sunday evenings in San Francisco there is a class devoted chiefly to a study of the Dharma Traditions. This is led by Wali Ali in the Mentorgarten garage, which has been converted into a meeting room for limited-sized groups. Dances and chants are performed using the sacred phrases from Hinduism and Buddhism, and Murshid Sam Lewis's Dharma-derived poetry as well as some forms of meditation are also given, the basic Jnanas of Lord Buddha being a mainstay.

Also at Mentorgarten is a public meeting in Sufism held Monday nights and led by Sheikh Wali Ali. The dances of Murshid Lewis are a liberally applied relief to the perhaps more mentally involved portions of study, although they themselves involve very deep moral, psychic, and spiritual unfoldment.

The climax of the week's events is the Wednesday night meeting in Sausalito held in a large gymnasium. The emphasis at this gathering is mainly on dancing. Since this is the one time of the week when all of the various groups are in attendance they are able to present an entire program, throughout which the members are able to experience a quite integrated presence of heart-life.

Sheikh Amin leads a practice each week at this meeting, usually a type of meditation.

Ala-ud-d-n Mathieu is the maestro. The choir he directs takes its expressions from all over this world, and no doubt from other higher worlds as well. They have worked with the Grateful Dead band on a number of occasions.

There is another meeting that Sheikh Amin directs in his Corte Madera home, The Garden of Allah. This meeting began several years ago as a simple get-together of disciples and personal friends but has developed steadily into a fine exploratory and practical form toward the understanding of the heart.

The work in Walk and Dance is chiefly the result of Murshid Sam Lewis's efforts to present to the world a Yoga of joyous activity in and toward God.

Although most of the disciples are of the late Murshid Sam Lewis there is an increasing association with the work of Pir Vilayat Khan.

For further information write to Mentorgarten, 410 Precita Ave., San Francisco, Calif. 94110.

SUFISM REORIENTED

Sufism Reoriented is a spiritual order and Sufi school presently under the direction of "Murshida" Ivy Oneita Duce. Tracing its history from the Western Sufi order established around the turn of the century by Hazrat Inayat Khan, the order was reoriented in 1952 by Meher Baba, considered by thousands as the Avatar or Christ of the age. There have always been Sufis who have allied themselves with the Avatar each time he has come. Meher Baba confirmed Ms. Duce's status as the Murshida of the order and gave her the responsibility of carrying on the Sufi teachings under his authority and guidance.

The order emphasizes "bhakti" (the path of love and selfless service) and the importance of developing true moral character for life in the world. Special attention is given to the guidance of Meher Baba and the necessity of faith and trust in the Murshida. Sufism Reoriented provides a system of inner training for those who wish to go beyond the formal side of religion and arrive at the real heart of spiritual life. Using various techniques of unfolding one's "real self," the Sufi school aims to guide "mureeds" (students) to the integration of true mysticism with life in the everyday world. As a universal approach to spirituality, Sufism Reoriented accepts aspirants of every race, religion, creed, and nationality.

There are regular meetings for members and introductory classes for sincere seekers. These introductory classes, which may be taken without obligation, have been held each autumn. Sufi instruction is personal and no correspondence courses are offered.

Sufism Reoriented is a major publisher of Meher Baba's works and the Sufi Center operates a bookstore. The Center also functions as a source of information about Meher Baba, Sufi studies, and Sufi authorities of the past. The order occasionally sponsors dramatic presentations and public lectures on Universal Truth. The Sufi Center office is usually open to visitors.

For further information, contact Sufism Reoriented, 1290 Sutter St., San Francisco, Calif. 94109; (415) 441–8101.

TIBETAN NYINGMAPA MEDITATION CENTER

In hopes of fulfilling the wish of his Guru—to bring an understanding of Tibetan Buddhism to the West—Tarthang Tulka Rinpoche traveled through Europe and America. Arriving in Berkeley in 1969, he established the Tibetan Nyingmapa Meditation Center. Here he teaches the fundamentals of Buddhist practice and philosophy. The master-disciple relationship is central to the transmission of a tradition. With the guidance of Rinpoche, the Nyingma tradition and practices can be preserved and transmitted in the West.

The Center publishes *Crystal Mirror*, a magazine that includes various articles on Tibet and India.

For further information contact Tibetan Nyingmapa Meditation Center, 2522 Webster St., Berkeley, Calif. 94705; (415) 549–1618.

THE UNIFICATION CHURCH

Conscientious people everywhere are realizing that man and his world are undergoing a spiritual as well as a physical revolution. Many proclaim this as the "Dawn of a New Age," the beginning of the Age of Aquarius, the emergence of a new and higher level of spiritual awareness. Man is becoming more and more aware of the need to actualize ideals that he has held from the dawn of his existence. But many have found it difficult if not impossible to reach these long-sought-after goals.

The Unification Church (Unified Family) claims to have discovered the most direct, realistic, and natural method of achieving these universal ideals. This method or Way is to be found in the Unification Principle, a teaching or philosophy that has grown out of a revelation received by the contemporary Korean spiritual Master, Sun Myung Moon. Centered around this understanding, the Unified Family has become a revolutionary, worldwide organism for spiritual and psychic transformation.

God need no longer be considered a mysterious and distant entity, but can now be seen and understood throughout the physical as well as spiritual realm. He now reveals Himself through science as well as mysticism, rationality as well as emotion, logic as well as intuition.

Members of this international Family live as brothers and sisters within closely knit communities, recognizing God as the Father and Mother of all. By learning and applying the guidelines of the Unification Principle, they create an intense spiritual atmosphere rich in potential for individual self-actualization and collective evolution. Through day-to-day living of "The Principle," each person can grow to completion, unfolding his or her intrinsic beauty and value as a flower opens its petals to the sun.

Unification Church centers are located in more than 30 countries around the world, with International Headquarters in Seoul, Korea. In the United States, there are five main centers: U.S. Headquarters, 1611 Upshur St., N.W., Washington, D.C. 20011; 1727 Euclid Ave., Berkeley, Calif. 94709; 4749 King St., New York, N.Y. 10014; 1760 Courtney Ave., Los Angeles, Calif. 90046; 770 Clarkson, Denver, Colo. 80218.

THE UNITED CHURCH OF RELIGIOUS SCIENCE

The United Church of Religious Science is a rapidly growing movement that teaches that God is within man and that practices spiritual mind treatment as scientific prayer, with answered prayer called Demonstrations. It is based on the religious philosophical teachings of Dr. Ernest Holmes, 1887–1960, author of *Science of Mind*.

"Religious Science," as defined by Dr. Holmes, "is a correlation of the laws of science, the opinions of philosophy, and the revelations of religion applied to human needs and the aspirations of man."

The International Headquarters of the United Church of Religious Science is located at 3251 W. Sixth St., Los Angeles, Calif. 90075, where it maintains a worldwide *Ministry of Prayer* (213) 388–2181 and where it also publishes the *Science of Mind* magazine, now in its 43rd year.

UNIVERSAL GREAT BROTHERHOOD

The Universal Great Brotherhood, founded by Dr. Serge Raynaud de la Ferriere, is an international, cultural, and Initiatic organization that works for the elevation of human thought by the union of science and religion. The U.G.B. promotes the union of all people regardless of race, creed, sex, social, or cultural level as well as the union of scientific, philosophical, spiritual, artistic, literary, recreational, and other organizations to form a field of universal synthesis and spiritual supremacy. The U.G.B. seeks world peace and brotherhood by means of having each individual attain peace within; hence, yoga is taught to help man achieve inner peace and spiritual growth.

Common establishments of the U.G.B. include Yoga Institutes, Cultural and Study Centers, Ashrams, the International University of the U.G.B. with its Superior Schools of Yoga and Cosmobiology and Lyceums of Synthesis, Universal Temples, Initiatic Colleges, libraries, and Kari Explorer scout groups. Lectures on various subjects in such fields as science, art, philosophy, comparative religions, psychology, metaphysics, esoterism, social welfare service, recreational, social, and artistic events are typical U.G.B. activities.

The U.G.B. is a nonprofit, nonpolitical and nonsectarian organization, with centers and interest groups in some thirty countries through the world. Centers in the United States are: Universal Great Brotherhood, 2408 24th St., San Francisco, Calif. 94110; (415) 824–0231; and G.P.O. Box 949, New York, N.Y. 10001.

VEDANTA SOCIETY OF SOUTHERN CALIFORNIA

Vedanta is the philosophy that has evolved from the teachings of the Vedas, a collection of ancient Indian scriptures, the oldest writings that exist in the world. More generally, the term "Vedanta" includes not only the Vedas themselves but the whole mass of literature that has developed from them right down to the present day.

Vedanta teaches three fundamental truths: 1. The Godhead, the underlying Reality, is omnipresent. Therefore, it must be within each one of us and within every creature and object. So man, in his true nature, is God. 2. It is the purpose of man's life on earth to unfold and manifest this Godhead, which is externally existent within him, but hidden. 3. Truth is universal. Men seek the Godhead in various ways, but what they seek is always the same.

The Vedanta Society of Southern California is a non-profit religious corporation with a membership of about five hundred. It has, in addition to the temple, a convent at Santa Barbara, and a monastery at Trabuco Canyon near Santa Ana.

The following quotation is from the Society's Amended Articles of Incorporation: "The purposes for which said corporation is formed are: a. To promote the study of the philosophy and religion of Vedanta. b. To promote harmony between Eastern and Western thought and recognition of the truth in all the great religions of the world." These purposes are pursued primarily by means of public lectures and classes held in Hollywood, Santa Barbara, and Trabuco, and through personal instruction in prayer and meditation. The Society also publishes a bimonthly magazine called *Vedanta and the West*, maintains three bookshops, and sponsors a number of pamphlet and book publications.

There are twelve other Vedanta organizations in America, Europe, and South America. While each center functions as an independent, self-supporting unit run by its own board of trustees, all are under the spiritual guidance of the Ramakrishna Order of India.

The Ramakrishna Path and Mission, as it is called, is a religious order founded in India in 1897 by Swami Vivekananda and other monastic disciples of the now universally revered Bengali saint of the late nineteenth century, Sri Ramakrishna, whose message was that "all religions are but different paths leading to the one goal—God."

For further information, or a list of other centers in America, write to Secretary, Vedanta Society of Southern California, 1946 Vedanta Pl., Hollywood, Calif. 90028; (213) 465–7114.

WAILUA UNIVERSITY

Wailua University of Contemplative Arts was conceived as a vehicle for the freeing and sustaining of man's inner being.

SRI RAMAKRISHNA

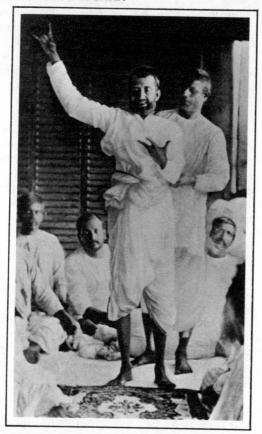

❝To attain God a man must
have certain favorable
conditions: the company
of holy men, discrimination,
and the blessings
of a real teacher.❞

It can be perceived as an extension of the same purpose and the same philosophy that created the Mystery Schools during the Golden Age of Greece. Pythagoras, Euclid, Plato, and Socrates taught not intellectual knowledge so much as they provided the atmosphere that allowed for the unfoldment of the whole man, from the inside out. Pythagoras, for example, required applicants to his school to fast for forty days before he accepted them; once they were accepted, they were immediately put on silence for five years.

Wailua University's requirements are not quite as severe. But the purpose remains the same. It is the unfolding of man's subtle inner consciousness, the refinement of his every fiber, and the ultimate experience of the Self, beyond the stilled mind, for which Wailua University was founded. The basic idea is that in his day-to-day life man can learn to express his inner being. He has many vehicles at his disposal. By developing such a contemplative life-style he hones his every moment, eventually shaping the tools and instruments that he needs to maintain his sublime and peaceful inner life.

The study at Wailua University is as much an unlearning as a learning process. It is a doing away with the primordial concepts of fear, greed, attachment, and anxiety. It is also the acquisition of new techniques of meditation, the sharpening of perception, and the development of greater and greater abilities of handling the daily, challenging situations.

Wailua University grows out of the idea that man is not simply a creature within an environment but rather that what surrounds him is a reflection of himself. Once he begins to study his own life he can simultaneously be aware and function in deep superconscious states and handle external activities and relationships with great facility and ease.

Wailua University of Contemplative Arts has campuses, schools, and monasteries in Alaveddy, Ceylon; Virginia City, Nevada; and San Francisco, California; and by one of the waterfalls of the Wailua River on the Garden Island of Kauai, in Hawaii.

For further information, write to Wailua University of

Contemplative Arts, Monastery and Administration, Kapaa on the Garden Island, Hawaii 96746.

THE YOU INSTITUTE—"A CENTER OF LIGHT"

The You Institute, founded in 1930 under the leadership of Dr. Jacques Hondorus, is dedicated to revealing the Cosmic Light through the understanding and application of the physical, mental, and spiritual laws of the Universe.

The You Institute is particularly concerned with the gradual training of its members into higher unfoldment, where the flow of peace and harmony combined with the deeper realizations of wisdom, awareness, energy, and mastery become the keys to self-fulfillment.

Predicated on the law of balance and continual rebirth, this meditation orientation is a direct way of Divine Realization and blissful abundance on all planes of existence.

For further information contact The You Institute, 1443 Colorado Blvd., Los Angeles, Calif. 90041; (213) 257–6429.

THE ZEN CENTER

The Zen Center in San Francisco has grown from a few students of Shunryu Suzuki Roshi to hundreds of students who regularly practice morning and evening meditation, attend lectures, and live according to the rules of a zendo.

Tassajara is the Zen Mountain Center also started by Suzuki Roshi. Located in Monterey County, California, it is the first Zen Buddhist monastery in the Americas. The monastery has fifty to sixty students, men and women, who practice zazen, the traditional Zen method of sitting meditation, and who follow a daily schedule that includes services and lectures, meals, work, bathing, and sleep. Students eat a comparatively simple diet consisting chiefly of grains, beans, vegetables, and fruits.

Tassajara is closed to the public during the winter months so that the formal practice periods may take place; it continues to accommodate guests during the summer months, May through September.

The Zen Center publishes a quarterly bulletin called

Wind Bell that offers lectures and information about affiliated centers and schedules of special programs.

In 1971 Shunryu Suzuki Roshi passed on. In the traditional Zen manner he prepared everything so that it would run smoothly in his absence. During his last days he used what little strength he had to lead a final sesshin. The new Roshi is Richard Baker who has lived and studied in Japan as well as with Suzuki Roshi.

For further information about the center or Tassajara write to Zen Center, 300 Page St., San Francisco, Calif. 94102.

ZEN MISSION SOCIETY

Shasta Abbey, located along the Shasta-Trinity National Forest in Northern California, is the headquarters for the Zen Mission Society and a Sōtō Zen Priesthood Training Monastery.

At present twenty-five people are undergoing the intensive training program of the monastery. They have come here because they are dissatisfied with the state they are in and wish to do something about it. The program of the Abbey is designed as a means to develop inner strength and positivity within the trainee so that he or she can return to the outside world and benefit others. There are both men and women here and all are free to marry. The program has been designed so that all will learn to live a completely normal life in the everyday world after training.

The origins of the Zen Mission Society began some ten years ago as the Foreign Guest Department of Sōjiji, one of the two head temples of the Soto Zen Buddhist Church in Japan. Its Chief Abbot, Kōhō Chisan Zenji, appointed Rev. Jiyu Kennett, an Englishwoman whom he had especially chosen for this work, as the Foreign Guest Master. After he had carefully trained her and then given her the Dharma Transmission it was her duty to instruct the hundreds of westerners who had come to Japan to study Zen. On Kōhō Zenji's death he wished her to come to the West to spread Buddhism and teach it in a western framework.

Kennett Rōshi was fully licensed to teach in 1968 by the

Sōtō Zen Headquarters Office. She is at present the Chief Priest and Abbess of Shasta Abbey.

For further information contact the Zen Mission Society, Shasta Abbey, Box 577, R.R. 1, Mount Shasta, Calif. 96067; (916) 926–4208.

PUBLICATIONS,
BOOK
STORES

AURORA BOOKSTORE

This store specializes in books on occultism, teaching of the East and West, psychology, New Age thought, Sri Aurobindo literature, incense, Tarot cards and posters from India.

Aurora Bookstore, 8 Mill Hill Rd., Woodstock, N.Y. 12498.

BACK TO GODHEAD

The magazine of the Hare Krishna Movement, *Back To Godhead* presents the transcendental science of God-realization known only to the saints of India's unbroken disciple succession.

It is published monthly by Iskon Press, a division of the International Society for Krishna Consciousness, Inc., 32 Tiffany Pl., Brooklyn, N.Y. 11231.

BANYEN BOOK SHOP

Banyen Book Shop is a mail-order book house for spiritual and related subjects.

For their catalog write to Banyen Book Shop, 2739 W. Fourth Ave., Vancouver 8, B.C., Canada.

BODHI TREE BOOKSTORE

This bookstore is very well stocked with spiritual esoteric, eastern religion, occult, astrology and other New Age publications. Many difficult to find books are on their shelves, especially in Buddhism, Yoga and Sufism. The Bodhi Tree offers free lectures by visiting swamis, gurus, authors, or other people of interest. It also offers several unusual things to its customers: complimentary cups of herb tea, comfortable chairs to sit in, incense, classical music and a pleasant atmosphere.

Bodhi Tree Bookstore, 8585 Melrose Avenue, West Hollywood, Calif. 90069 (213) 659–1733.

BIG ROCK CANDY MOUNTAIN

Big Rock Candy Mountain is a vehicle for communication among people concerned with education, both personal and public. Materials and books have no inherent power by themselves. Only people using, experiencing, and learning with these aids give them meaning. Techniques, work-in-progress, classroom and personal applications and evaluations appear with their usual reviews in each of the quarterly issues.

Big Rock Candy Mountain is published by the Portola Institute. A subscription is $8 a year.

Big Rock Candy Mountain, 1115 Merrill St., Menlo Park, Calif. 94025.

BIG SUR RECORDINGS

Big Sur Recordings develops archives and produces and distributes recordings for Esalen Institute and other centers of research into man's positive possibilities. Each title is recorded live at the time of the event.

For a catalog listing their recorded tapes write to Big Sur Recordings, P.O. Box 4119, San Rafael, Calif. 94903.

CHAKRA

Chakra is a nonprofit journal dedicated to Tantra and Yoga. Contributors enjoy full liberty and retain copyright of their articles.

Chakra is published by Kumar Gallery, 11 Sundar Nagar Market, New Delhi 3, India, and can be purchased at most bookstores that stock New Age publications.

CITY LIGHTS BOOKSTORE

City Lights carries a selection of books dealing with the New Age. They usually know what's going on in the Bay Area.

City Lights Bookstore, 261 Columbus Ave., San Francisco, Calif. 94133.

CLEAR CREEK

"Wherever You Live, A Clear Creek Belongs There." Clear Creek is an environmental newspaper published monthly by Clear Creek, 617 Mission St., San Francisco, Calif. 94105.

THE COOPERATOR

The Cooperator is a bimonthly, joint publication of the International Cooperation Council and The Cooperators. It aims to share the key ideas and concerns of our time that lead toward a new civilization based upon "unity in diversity among all peoples." *The Cooperator* seeks to represent the organizations within and related to ICC as well as possible and in so doing aims to rouse people from their inertia, their complacency, and their resignation to the state of their world.

For additional information contact 17819 Roscoe Blvd., Northridge, Calif. 91324.

CRYSTAL MIRROR

Crystal Mirror is a periodical of the Tibetan Nyingmapa Meditation Center of Berkeley, California. It is designed to serve as a means of communication between the Center and the community and as a source of information for those interested in Tibetan Buddhism and Tibetan culture.

Dharma Publishing, P.O. Box 4060, Berkeley, Calif. 94704.

DE VORSS & COMPANY

Distributors, since 1929, of an extensive line of books dealing with metaphysics, occultism, religion, science of mind, theosophy, healing, and self-improvement. The DeVorss catalog offers books selected from the listings of approximately 200 publishers and book suppliers. Retail sales by mail order only; wholesale to bookstores, churches, and public libraries. DeVorss & Company also publishes over a hundred titles, including the books formerly handled by The Farallon Foundation, Huna Research (Max Freedom Long), Scrivener & Co., and The Goldsmith Book Center. The DeVorss catalog, including a Subject Guide, is available *free of charge*.

DeVorss & Company, 1641 Lincoln Blvd., Santa Monica, Calif. 90404; (215) 451–0660; (213) 870–7470.

THE EARTH GUILD

Six months after the Grateful Union Book Store opened, the group found that there was still more energy to channel and they opened The Earth Guild, a beautiful, soft-vibed crafts, supplies, and bookstore. Again the store became more than a store. As Rick, one of the backbones of the family, says, "We consider life itself a craft and an art, therefore we have books on everything from weaving and pottery all the way to plumbing, wiring, carpentry, and gardening." There is a plentiful stock of weaving materials, candle and fabric dyes, beading, and pottery.

The group is continually growing and evolving, and is an example of how to really live a New Age life-style in the present world. According to Rick, the source of understanding for this group and their work is that "We all see, in one way or another, that everybody is all there is, and the best way to get here is to be who you are."

The Earth Guild, 149 Putnam Ave., Cambridge, Mass. 02139.

EAST WEST JOURNAL

East West Journal is the newspaper for the macrobiotic community and all those interested in the food they eat.

East West Journal, P.O. Box 203, Prudential Center Station, Boston, Mass. 02199.

ESCOPE

Escope-Esoteric Scope is a magazine published bimonthly by the House of Manna, a nonprofit corporation. Its purpose is to express both the spiritual and physical aspects of the project of the House by expounding the Sufistic philosophy extended in its activity.

House of Manna, The Zaouia, 8003 Hollywood Blvd., Los Angeles, Calif. 90046.

EVERYBODY'S BOOKSHOP

317 Sixth St.
Los Angeles, Calif. 90014

FIELDS BOOKSHOP

Fields has an extensive selection of spiritual books and publications of related subjects. If you are interested in the ideas of Gurdjieff, this is a good place to visit. There is also a lovely garden for meditation.

Fields Bookshop, 1419 Polk St., San Francisco, Calif. 94109.

GARUDA

Garuda presents the teachings of Tibetan Buddhism and the work of Chogyma Trangpa Rinpoche. Future issues will include the works of distinguished religious and lay teachers, scholars, and artists.

According to the Indian myth, the Garuda is the celestial hawk who hatches from the egg fully developed. In this sense, he symbolizes the awakened state of mind, Buddha-nature. He destroys and eats the five nagas of snakes, which represent the diseases, both physical and psychological, to which all beings are prey. In his middle he holds the Bodhi leaf, symbolic of the Hinayana. In the center of the Bodhi leaf is the knot of eternity, the indestructible quality of meditation and its discovery of sunyata, which indicates the Mahayana. Above his head is a vajra, representing the Vajrayana. The sun represents skillful means and compassion. The Tibetan quotation that the Garuda holds in his claws is from the Sutra of Manjushri and translates as "The proclamation of truth is fearless."

Garuda is published by Tail of the Tiger and Karma Dzong centers.

For information write to Tail of the Tiger, Star Route, Barnet, Vt. 05821; or Karma Dzong, Salina Star Route, Boulder, Colo. 80302.

GILBERT'S BOOKSHOP

6278 Hollywood Blvd.
Hollywood, Calif. 90028

GOTHAM BOOK MART

The Gotham Book Mart has a fine selection of spiritual books. This section is run by Frances Stelloff, a lovely white-haired lady who has abundant knowledge about any of the books stacked from the floor in her area. The books are always there; Ms. Stelloff is usually there in the afternoon.

41 W. 47th St.
New York, N.Y. 10036; (212) PLaza 7–0367

GRATEFUL UNION BOOK STORE

This center for psychological and metaphysical reading materials is far more than just a bookstore. It began a few years ago out of the vision of a commune of eight people who had come together to live and work on themselves. Seeking a way of utilizing energies, doing something worthwhile, and making a living, the "family" opened a well-stocked bookstore containing the kind of books that interested them. The store has since become an information center for the spiritual circuit around Cambridge, as well as a good place to hang out with some conversation and books.

The Grateful Union Book Store, 1124 Massachusetts Ave., Cambridge, Mass. 02138; (617) 868–9637.

MASON'S BOOKSHOP

Astrology classes and a good selection of spiritual books are featured here.

Mason's Bookshop, 789 Lexington Ave., New York, N.Y. 10021; (212) 832–8958.

H.E.L.P. UNLIMITED

Warren and Jo Stag run this restaurant, bookstore, market, and Hall of Help. The restaurant and market serve organic foods and the bookstore specializes in spiritual, New Age books and magazines, with a section on natural foods and diet. The Hall of Help has lectures and classes on nutrition, yoga and related subjects.

For more information contact H.E.L.P. Unlimited, 7910 W. Third St., Los Angeles, Calif. 90048; (213) 653–4357.

METAPHYSICAL ASTROLOGICAL TOWNHALL BOOKSHOP

Publications on the Aquarian Age, esoteric lectures, and esoteric classes can be found here.

Metaphysical Astrological Townhall Bookshop, 345 Mason St., San Francisco, Calif. 94102.

METAPHYSICAL CENTER & BOOKSTORE

420 Sutter St.
San Francisco, Calif. 94102

KRISHNAMURTI FOUNDATION BULLETIN

A quarterly publication sent to donors of the Krishnamurti Foundation of America, P.O. Box 216, Ojai, California 93023. It contains information with respect to speaking schedules of J. Krishnamurti in the United States and throughout the world, his latest publications and recordings, and carries a hitherto unpublished writing or talk by Krishnamurti.

Krishnamurti books and recordings are available through the Krishnamurti Foundation for retail trade only.

METROPOLITAN LECTURE CALENDAR

The Metropolitan Lecture Calendar is an information service of the International Center for Integrative Studies. It is a selection of lectures dealing with the central issues of man, and lists lectures and workshops on such subjects as poetry, group encounters, Yoga, growth centers, and psychology. This calendar covers events in and around the New York area.

For more information contact International Center for Integrative Studies, 142 W. Houston St., New York, N.Y. 10012; (212) 477–7340.

THE MODERN UTOPIAN

The Modern Utopian is a paperback magazine published by Alternative Foundations, P.O. Drawer A, San Francisco, Calif. 94131.

Write for information about membership in Alternatives.

NATURAL LIFE STYLES

As the title implies, it is a guide to organic living.

Natural Life Styles, P.O. Box 150, New Paltz, N.Y. 12561.

NOT MAN APART

Not Man Apart is a monthly newspaper dealing with the environment and the challenge to live in it successfully.

For information, write to Friends of the Earth, 8016–G Zuni Rd., S.E., Albuquerque, N.M. 87108.

THE ORDER OF THE UNIVERSE

The Order of the Universe is a macrobiotic magazine that aims to study spiritual development in relation to diet. It attempts to establish a principle to unify modern science and ancient intuitive wisdom. Articles include acupuncture, Oriental religion, "introspective medicine," perennial philosophy, nutrition, and related subjects. According to this publishing group, "We do not seek spiritual development, but a world in which spiritual development becomes unnecessary."

Offices are located at 295 Huntington Ave., Boston, Mass. 02115.

ORIENTALIA, INC.

Books on Eastern wisdom
61 Fourth Ave.
New York, N.Y. 10003; (212) 473–6730.

THE PILGRIM'S WAY

The Pilgrim's Way offers an extensive selection of metaphysical books. In a pleasant browsers' atmosphere, there are books on astrology, Oriental philosophy, religion, psychology, magic, Qabalah, alchemy, Sufism, Yoga, Zen and Tarot. You can purchase incense, Tarot cards, a mala, or have an interesting talk with Devi Davies, who owns the shop.

The Pilgrim's Way, Dolores near Sixth, P.O. Box 1944, Carmel, Calif. 93921.

SHAMBALA BOOK SELLERS

2482 Telegraph Pl.
San Francisco, Calif. 94133

THE SOURCE

The Source, owned and run by Jim Baker, is a health food restaurant that offers dining both indoors and outdoors. On a wall inside is this sign: "I AM, HIS SOUL, HIS SOUL AND I ARE ONE." Behind the restaurant is a kutir (meditation hut) where meditations are given every evening exactly at 6 P.M.

For more information, contact The Source, 8301 Sunset Blvd., Los Angeles, Calif. 90069; (213) 656–6388.

SPHINX SELF EXPLORATION BOOK SHOP

The Sphinx carries an abundant and consciously selected stock of books on "the path," ranging from astrology, Tarot, the Occult through psychology and on to Christian mystics and Eastern teachings. The shop offers good music, empty chairs and hot tea.

Sphinx Self Exploration Book Shop, 111 Mount Auburn St., Cambridge, Mass. 02138; (617) 491–8788.

SRI SATHYA SAI BABA BOOK CENTER OF AMERICA

This shop specializes in books and publications on Sathya Sai Baba.

For information contact Sri Sathya Sai Baba Book Center of America, P.O. Box 278, Tustin, Calif. 92680, Attention: W. R. Cowan.

SUFIS SPEAK

Dedicated to those who have held aloft the light of truth through the darkness of human ignorance, this newsletter is sent out once a month to those who request it. It aims to give those who are far from a center a tie with Sufi events in all parts of the world.

For information write to Sufis Speak, P.O. Box 7168, Seattle, Wash. 98133.

TAO BOOKS AND PUBLICATIONS, INC.

Primarily an outlet for macrobiotic and related works, Tao stocks a limited but valuable supply of other Eastern reading material. The store is also an informal center for the macrobiotic community.

Tao Books and Publications, Inc., 303B Newbury St., Boston, Mass. 02115; (617) 487–8399.

THREE RINGS BOOKSTORE

This little bookshop, located on the wharf in Monterey, is packed with a selection of New Age books and a fine selection of publications on related subjects. Coffee and tea are available and you can look through a book while comfortably seated.

Three Rings Bookstore, Fisherman's Wharf No. 1, Monterey, Calif. 93940.

TIMELESS OCCULT BOOKSHOP

8201 Sunset Blvd.
Hollywood, Calif. 90046

SAMUEL WEISER

This is the largest and best stocked bookstore in the world which specializes in the occult, astrology, Gurdjieff, New Age publications, and all spiritual and related subjects.

In 1968, Weiser began publishing the kind of books they sell and have become one of the largest publishers of this type of book. It is an experience to visit this store where so many books of a spiritual nature are stacked from floor to ceiling.

Samuel Weiser, 734 Broadway, New York, N.Y. 10003 (212) GRamercy 7–8453.

THE WHOLE EARTH CATALOG

"The Whole Earth Catalog functions as an evaluation and access device. With it, the user should know better what is worth getting and where and how to do the getting.

"We are as gods and might as well get good at it. So far remotely done power and glory—as via government, big business, formal education, church—have succeeded to the point where gross defects obscure actual gains. In response to this dilemma and to these gains a realm of intimate, personal power is developing, the power of the individual to conduct his own education, find his own inspiration, shape his own environment, and share his adventure with whomever is interested. Tools that aid this process are sought and promoted by *The Whole Earth Catalog*."

The Whole Earth Catalog, 1115 Merrill St., Menlo Park, Calif. 94025.

THE WOODSTOCK AQUARIAN

Group Consciousness, Tribal Consciousness, Spaceship Earth—these are the concerns of the New Age and *The Woodstock Aquarian*. Everything in this publication is part of a wheel. The content is many-faceted, like the spokes in a wheel. It all comes together at the hub. The hub is empty. It represents you . . . me . . . us . . . everyone . . . and It.

The Woodstock Aquarian is published quarterly by Great Turtle Enterprises, Inc. They also have a mail order catalog.

The Woodstock Aquarian, Box 401, Woodstock, N.Y. 12498.

YOGA BOOK STORE

Open afternoons and by appointment, The Yoga Book Store specializes in recent and old books on Yoga. It also has many scarce and out-of-print occult books.

Yoga Book Store, 80 E. 11th St., New York, N.Y. (212) 674–7440.

72 73 74   12 11 10 9 8 7 6 5 4 3 2 1